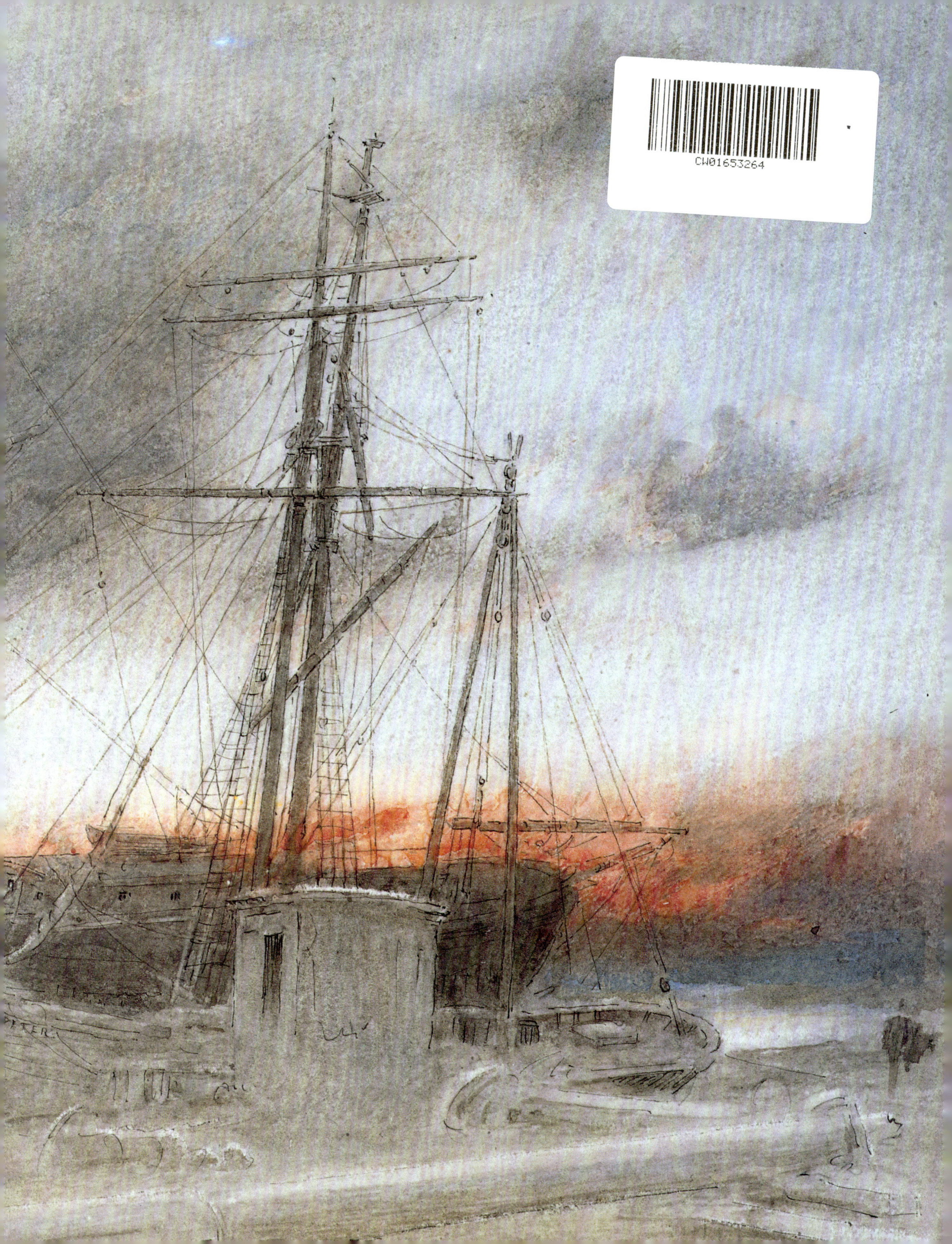

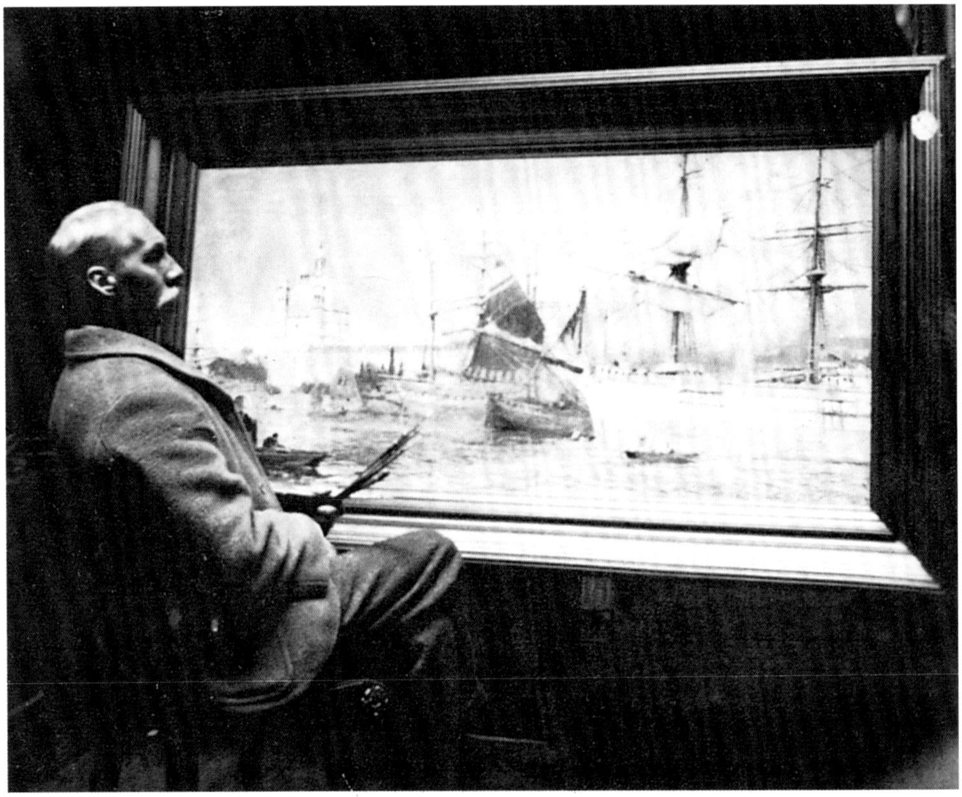

Albert Goodwin before *The Hardy Norseman in Venice*

Exhibited at the Royal Academy 1920, no 600
(the last work Goodwin exhibited at the RA)

ALBERT GOODWIN RWS 1845-1932

Chris Beetles Limited

Chris Beetles Gallery
8 & 10 Ryder Street
London
SW1Y 6QB

Telephone 020 7839 7551
Fax 020 7839 1603
E-mail gallery@chrisbeetles.com
Website www.chrisbeetles.com

ISBN: 978-1-905738-02-1

Edited by Fiona Nickerson
Exhibition details researched by Phil Tite
Designed by The Bridgewater Book Company
Printing by BAS Printers

Cover: Blakeney, Norfolk (no 115)
Front endpapers: The Shipbreakers Yard (no 95)
Back endpapers: Palma, Majorca (no 127)
Back cover: Lincoln (no 82)

WHY ALBERT GOODWIN MATTERS

By Godfrey Barker

Goodwin, born in 1845, arrived on the Victorian landscape scene when the shadow of J M W Turner began to fall long upon it. The elevation of Turner as the sun-god of Victorian art was the passionate mission of Ruskin[i] and Ruskin's elevation of Turner, alongside his elevation of the Pre-Raphaelites, created difficulties for every artist after 1870 who wished to paint in subtler tones than the brilliance of Holman Hunt and the dazzling yellows preferred by Turner[ii]. (Ruskin, as Goodwin complained in his diary, had lowered the public esteem of that subtler colourist, John Constable.) The towering status of Turner as genius of the century raised problems not only for Goodwin but for other watercolourists, for such independent spirits as Allingham, Birket Foster, Brabazon, Inchbold, Palmer, Richardson, even Whistler. How to be individual in the glare of such a man? How to build on Turner's achievement, yet escape from him?

There was a second prison from which Goodwin felt the need to escape - an artistic cell to which he was confined by John Ruskin.

Ruskin, with his conviction that form mattered more than colour, commanded Goodwin in his youth that the artist must always choose for his subject a scene or an object of beauty - that is, a subject beautiful in its own right. In Victorian England, where the landscape changed dramatically every day under the weight of heavy industry and the blue sky turned to smoky grey, this requirement ruled out an enormous number of subjects. The Ruskin rule in effect condemned the artist to paint something other than what lay before him - to escape from ugly modern life to scenes more beautiful, to escape, in old-fashioned language, to the ideal world that was inhabited by painters from Raphael to Sir Joshua Reynolds. In a phrase, Ruskin forbade the existence of 'Contemporary Art' - or much, if not all of it.

Goodwin's diaries make clear that he chafed at this. He envied Whistler, who expressed public contempt for Ruskin, and he envied the freedom Whistler felt to paint the ugly and to be expressionist about it. In some diary entries, Goodwin openly admired Whistler, feeling him to be more correct about colour than Ruskin was about form.

Which way to go? Forcing himself to choose, Goodwin backed the 19th century, declaring Ruskin to be 'the truer wisdom' (*Diary*, 29 December 1914). He decided this when Ruskin was out of date in a 20th century that has elevated the ugly. Goodwin, in his grave, may nourish the hope that in the 21st Century he, Ruskin and the concept of beauty will steam back into fashion - that ugliness has run its course with the ultra-democratic art history of our time.

The escape of Albert Goodwin from Turner and Ruskin, the lifetime journey that he made to a style maturely and unmistakably his own, was not an easy one.

> I sometimes wonder if the spirit of old Turner takes over my personality. I often find (or think I find) myself doing the very same things that he seemed to do.[iii]

That is no more than a reference to Goodwin using spare paint on the palette at the end of one picture to start a new one but it announces the eternal presence of Turner in his mind. Hammond Smith, Goodwin's first and chief biographer, claims that his admiration for Turner was more present in his post-1900 work than at any other time,

> in his poetic and atmospheric use of colour, in his delicate and much more sensitive use of the pen, but most especially perhaps in his ability to combine a feeling for breadth with an eye for detail, which was such an unique feature of Turner's work.[iv]

One sees why he says this: lay Turner's *Fort Vimieux* of 1831 alongside a 1914 Goodwin sunset and it does look as if little has happened in between. Turner's rendering of vast, glowing abstract areas of colour in the 1835-40 oils and watercolours is undoubtedly faithfully reproduced in many Goodwin works. And yet Goodwin can be easily distinguished from Turner. How?

The answer seems to be that Turner is the truer Impressionist of the two - more concerned to lay down the truth of 'atmosphere' than to provide information of what is seen. The late Victorian Goodwin differed from Turner by his increasing interest in the subject, by thrusting topography into the viewer's face - even in openly atmospheric attempts like *The Lights of Lauterbrunnen* in 1919, which owes much to the late Turner Swiss views but tells us far more. Goodwin does this even in unashamed imaginations like the mood music *Benares*, a view of 1917 which the artist never saw in the moonlight in which he painted it and which is for many his masterpiece.

Goodwin's struggle, documented in the diaries, to be his own man and not the prisoner of Turner had one unusual consequence. It is that a majority of his most assured and individual work dates from his last twenty years.

To be at your best, imaginatively and technically, near your end is an unusual feat for any artist. Yet Goodwin's diaries reveal that he was thinking more intensely about painting in his 70s and 80s than at any other point of his life - and his work visibly burgeoned under his thought. What was swirling in his head in the 1910s and 1920s was not, however, a debate about the modern movement. It is a debate between Victorian dilemmas[v]. Goodwin has nothing to say about Picasso, Matisse, Modigliani, Cubism and the new directions of art, though in August 1909 he tells his diary that much Impressionism is 'laziness' and 'scamping on detail'. Paris, though not too far from Bexhill, was a world away in mind. So too is Ascot, Berkeley Square and the Roaring Twenties. Goodwin was to his end a Victorian and if he did his best work after 1900 Victorian England was still a powerful and enduring influence and Turner still a god.

To those who believe that art before 1925 is the rise of the school of Paris and the irrelevance or decease of all 19th century talent, including Goodwin, this judgment may come as a surprise.

But it is true. Along with Soames Forsyte in Galsworthy's great novel, Goodwin was one of many Victorians who survived long into the 20th century. As in *The Forsyte Saga*, Victorian conviction did not lie down and die with the death of the Queen in 1901. It continued to exist and make strong opinions felt about the decadence of Edwardian Europe and early 20th century art. And should any reader assume that Turner was somehow passé with the public in the age when Kandinsky and Picasso began work, the reverse is true: Turner was high fashion, and so was Albert Goodwin. On the art market, from the £5,250 cost of Turner's *Walton Bridges* in 1872, there is a rise of 1500% in forty years - in a gold standard age of roughly constant money - to the £30,800 paid by Henry Clay Frick for *Mortlake Terrace* in 1913. Turner was second only to Raphael and Gainsborough in world art prices when Goodwin filled his diary with esteem before the First World War. The Turner followers rose equally fast in value over the same period.

This has some bearing on the issue of Goodwin and the modern movement. Art historians - not least Frances Spalding in her *Dictionary of 20th Century Painters and Sculptors* - tend to write Goodwin (and many other Victorians who survived after 1900) out of the record. The judgment, a teleological one, is that the painters who mattered in the early 20th Century are those whom art historians prize in 2007. There is an alternative view as to who matters: the judgment of the age in which the artist lived. Albert Goodwin, as much as J M W Turner, was high fashion.

Art historians are writers who point telescopes at the past to advance the genius that they believe in. Their judgment makes some artists forward-looking and fashionable and others *passé*. Life is not like that. In his time, Goodwin was the future and the fashion. So was Turner. Picasso and the modern movement were not. Art history is just one type of selection of who matters and what matters, as vulnerable itself to dismissal in the name of fashion as the artists it rejects. That Goodwin painted alongside Picasso and Matisse, that he lived into the age of T S Eliot and *The Waste Land* - oddly, he and Eliot might have conversed well - is just one of those complexities that the impossible 20th Century has to take into account.

Fashion and art history are transient things. What endures is art creation and merit.

It matters not that in the definition of Frances Spalding and certain art historians, Goodwin was not 'of his time' or century after 1905, to use that imprisoning phrase of Baudelaire which has so limited the judgments of art history. And it is simply wrong to dismiss him - or any other artist - as part of a Victorian past that, at a thunderclap, became dead on the spot in 1901 and was without further relevance.

Life is not so tidy and this is simply bad history. Goodwin did important work on either side of the First World War, and during it. His most personal pictures of this time have a value which is considerably understated in 2007. That understatement also means that his 21st century price is absurdly low.

So how are we to praise Albert Goodwin? The Maidstone prodigy did not go short in his own time. His first painting to be acclaimed reached the Royal Academy by age 15, as did Turner's. Ruskin, who gave Goodwin a first Grand Tour of Europe, complete with culture shocks, in 1872, made him a favourite son and saluted his 'pure aesthetic delight'.

There is much to praise in this Beetles show; there are fine things like *Westminster* (1922, no 121), *Beachy Head* (1920, no 116) and *The Gardens, Pallanza, Lake Maggiore* (1915, no 106) which tell us much.

Goodwin possessed an extraordinary gift for modelling landscape with the sponge in single colours and lower and lower tones, using the pen to delineate form during and at the end of the process, never at the start. After Turner, no other watercolourist laid down giant zones of abstract colour with such sureness. It looks to be effortless; but when Lord Clark - Sir Kenneth Clark - went sketching with Goodwin in 1913 and 1914 and sought to imitate his methods, which Clark usefully describes, he achieved only 'mechanical' results.

Stare too, here at Goodwin's use of grey - in *Lincoln Canal* (1926, no 124) or the two views of *Palma, Majorca* (1925, nos 125 and 127) - the colour most important in his palette by 1910, into which he deliberately retreated and which he used to highlight the adjacent tones. Goodwin disliked 'the comparative deadness of Nature' in the Victorian palette but achieved his high colour by contrasts, placing grey alongside bright tints rather than resorting to the shrieking colours of Expressionism[vi]. Grey is a quiet colour, but it realised his aim. 'Actual reticence [is] far more subtle and beautiful', Goodwin confides to his diary in 1909, than 'Pre-Raphaelite superlatives'.

Then, for surprise, note the startling visual angles from which Goodwin often works.

This is not a man content, as were the mass of Victorian topographers, with the banality of the level horizon, with inchoate groping at the picturesque and sublime by snapshots up to misty mountain-tops. *Beachy Head* is painted from a steep and plunging Japanese point of vision. Often, too, his compositions shift the main focus of the painting one plane to the side, so that the harbour at *Bristol* (1901, no 76; an example among many) is an afterthought to much detail of telegraph poles, barrows, barge boys and shipping masts. Goodwin, among artists, was uniquely fond of scaffolding which he uses to conceal the main interest in *Lincoln Canal* and in five dozen other views - even his paintings of cathedrals.

Is Goodwin an Impressionist? He gets no mention in Laura Wortley's rewarding 1988 book on *British Impressionism* but then we must get down to basic definitions, French and English.

When Wynford Dewhurst asserted in 1904 that Impressionism was rooted in the English landscape tradition, he drew an angry response from Pissarro. Pissarro came to London with Monet in 1870 and spent much time in the National Gallery and the V & A with Gainsborough, Constable and Turner. 'This Mr Dewhurst understands nothing', Pissarro responded. What he and Monet found in the landscapes of Gainsborough was plein-air light and fugitive effects, what they found in Turner were errors and imperfections: 'his analysis of shadow... is ... a mere absence of light', his tone division was present but incorrect. For the true Impressionist, runs the message, the treatment of shadow is the thing that matters: shadow is light of a different quality and colour. It is not laid down with blacks and browns and earth tints, it is not the product of neutral shades and half-tones but it displays and is built up with the pure colours of the spectrum. Shadow is the great advance buried in Impressionism - the advance, if you like, between Manet's *Music in the Tuileries* in 1863 and Monet's *Impression: Sunrise* in 1874.

A true Impressionist painting, Pissarro might also have added, is an expression of mood rather than a document of a time or a place.

This definition I append to exclude much American plein-air painting, 1890-1920, from Impressionism. But the very thought floats upon a sea of confusion, for English art critics were once disposed to hail any landscape of mood or 'atmosphere' as 'Impressionist'.

Where do all these definitions leave Goodwin? His shadows seem to gain light and colour as early as 1884. But working in watercolour, he does not divide tone. Many of his pictures are documents but, like Turner's, many are not. The truth is that Goodwin painted numerous Impressionist pictures but he also painted many that are not. Most of his 'Impressionism' was done far from Britain in countries where the light invites, but he was 'Impressionist' also at home painting sunsets on the seashore; his chief interest was the mood of clouds and the sinking sun (much analysed in the diaries, especially in the wartime years). Goodwin painted much, right up to the end of his life, which in no way meets Pissarro's definition. But he would gratify the definitions of Philip Wilson Steer, who declared in 1891 to the Art Workers' Guild that Impressionism had existed since the frieze of the Parthenon and represented any poetic rather than factual treatment of a scene.

Albert Goodwin defies any easy analysis. His life was a struggle to escape artistic pigeon-holes. He followed the precepts of Turner and Ruskin but admired Whistler. He is sometimes an Impressionist, sometimes not. He was trained by Pre-Raphaelites, stayed loyal to the 'truth' they asserted, but ultimately deserted them. What is constant is the pleasure and deep reward he gave to his contemporaries and which he continues to give now.

i Until 1867 the highly descriptive Clarkson Stanfield was more expensive than Turner on the art market.

ii 'Turner's favourite colour was yellow... It's curious, of the three it's the one I least care for' (*Diary*, 9 January 1912).

iii *Diary*, 1911, quoted Hammond Smith, Albert Goodwin RWS, page 25

iv loc cit

v In 1915 Goodwin agonises over too much primary colour ('Nature does not fling crude paint about'), in 1918 he espouses, with guilt and uncertainty, tinted paper; in 1926 he is uneasy at working in pen on a semi-dry watercolour and harks back to the arguments of the 1870s about the introduction of bodycolour.

vi 'The flinging about of crude paints' is denounced in the *Diary* in 1915.

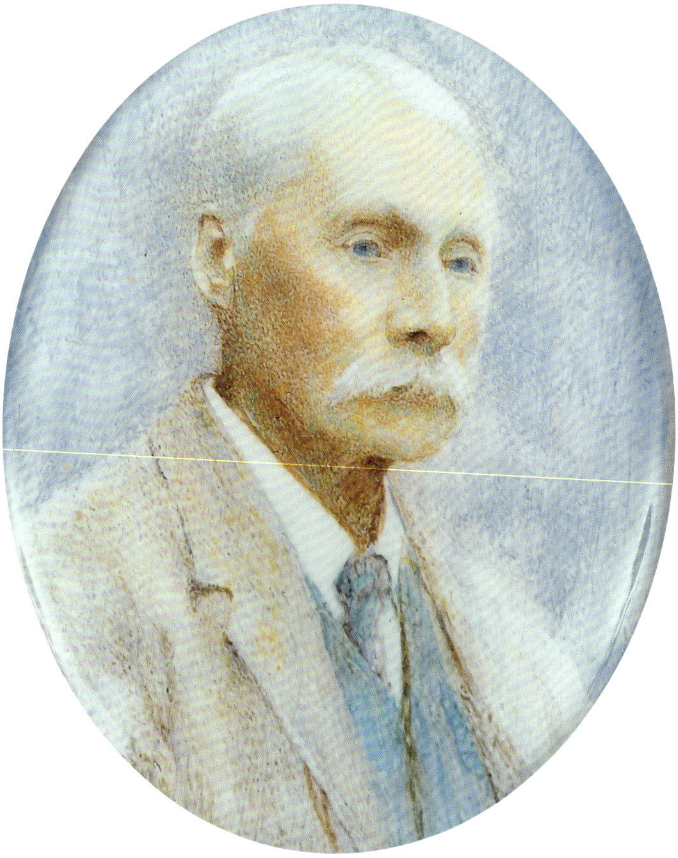

Albert Goodwin circa 1910
by his daughter Edytha.
watercolour miniature on ivory

HIS LIFE AND WORK

By Hammond Smith
Author and Biographer of *Albert Goodwin*, Leigh-on-Sea: F Lewis, 1977

'It is a great relief in an exhibition like this', wrote the art critic of *The Spectator* in his review of the RWS Winter Exhibition of 1881, 'which is mainly one of the disciplined skill exerted in somewhat commonplace directions, to turn to pictures like Mr Goodwin's, wherein the poetic feeling is so strong as to make us forget the technical skill which the artist possesses'.

Albert Goodwin had shown himself to be an artist with an individual vision from an early age, exhibiting his first picture at the Royal Academy[i], when he was just fifteen years old; and when he was still only nineteen years old, his master, Ford Madox Brown, writing to James Leathart, a patron of the Pre-Raphaelites, praised the work of his young pupil, predicting that 'there can be no doubt of his becoming before long one of the greatest landscape painters of the age'[ii]. Although it may be debatable whether Goodwin ever quite attained the pinnacle of distinction predicted by Brown, his work, which has an unmistakable character of its own, has rarely ceased to attract admirers and patrons, of whom the most distinguished was undoubtedly John Ruskin. Moreover, contemporary reviews of his work exhibited at the RWS in the 1870s and 1880s, variously refer to him as being 'the most imaginative member of the society'[iii]; as 'still the most interesting of the landscape painters here, and he is almost the only one in whom landscape receives any touch of ideal quality'[iv]; and 'he stands quite alone in his power of imparting a touch of fairy influence to his landscapes'[v].

Albert Goodwin was born in Maidstone[vi] in 1845, just three years before the Pre-Raphaelite Brotherhood was founded, and two years after the publication of Ruskin's first volume of *Modern Painters*. These dates are significant because it was in the artistic circles generated by Ruskin and the Pre-Raphaelites that Goodwin developed as an artist - first in the studio of Arthur Hughes, then under the supervision of F M Brown, and finally as a protégé of Ruskin. Although the Pre-Raphaelites were not primarily landscape painters, their views on 'truth to nature', and their practice of working directly from nature for the landscape settings of their pictures, inevitably influenced most contemporary landscape painters in the 1850s and 1860s; and in his *Notes on Prout and Hunt*, Ruskin quite rightly described Goodwin's work as having been 'founded first on strong Pre-Raphaelite veracities...'[vii]. Goodwin was, in fact, extremely fortunate in being taught by Brown, who is by far the most original and interesting of the landscape painters associated with the Pre-Raphaelite circle; however, despite Brown's devotion to the concept of truth to nature, and working *sur le motif*, his landscapes are, in the final analysis, strangely artificial - reminiscent of the magical realism of Palmer's Shoreham period rather than the naturalism of Constable, Cox or De Wint. Similarly, Goodwin's landscapes are invariably infused with a poetic charm that raises them above mere description; indeed, one critic complimented him for having that 'peculiar faculty of painting a natural scene with an undercurrent of supernatural feeling'[viii].

As a young artist, it was natural that Goodwin should have been attracted to what was considered the avant-garde art of his day, and his early work shows a Pre-Raphaelite concern for detail and for bright, clear colour. An important factor in Goodwin's approach to landscape painting, was his belief that it was a kind of religious activity, and that his own talents as a painter were God-given - views not unlike those held by Ruskin and some members of the Pre-Raphaelite circle.

'Let me not,' he wrote in his *Diary*,

> underestimate the gift God has given me...and in its measure this pleasure is passed along to those who know my work...Beauty - the beauty that is in the landscape - is a sealed book to many, hence in a degree the landscape painter may magnify his calling, for is he not one who is helping to open the eyes of the blind that they may see the hand of our Heavenly Father in the things that he has made for our delight?[ix]

However, the Pre-Raphaelites were not the only source of inspiration in the artistic development of Goodwin; more important perhaps for the development of his mature style was Turner - and the link between Turner, the Pre-Raphaelites and Goodwin was, of course, Ruskin. Goodwin met Ruskin towards the end of the 1860, probably as a result of his association with Hughes and Brown, and during the next few years, a friendship developed between them[x], with Goodwin holidaying with Ruskin at Abingdon and Matlock in 1871, and then in the following year, Goodwin spent three months touring Italy with Ruskin and another one of his protégés, Arthur Severn[xi] [see pages 24-32]. The relationship with Ruskin was of considerable importance to Goodwin, as until then he had paid little attention to drawing, but had been noted as an artist with 'an originality and courage in...the use of his paint box'[xii]. Now, under the guidance of Ruskin, he began to pay more attention to drawing, noting some years later that,

> I owe much thanks to Ruskin, who ballyragged me into love of form when I was getting too content with colour alone: and colour alone is luxury...how much I enjoyed the three months I had when I took up with drawing when with Ruskin in Italy; and how good it was for one. The pleasure that is to be found in *lines* which should string a drawing together is almost an unknown quantity in these days of paint and paint only.[xiii]

Although it was Ruskin who made Goodwin show a greater concern for drawing, and who encouraged him in the development of his sensitive use of the pen, it was the example of Turner who above all liberated the genius of Albert Goodwin. Ruskin himself had no difficulty in reconciling his admiration for the Pre-Raphaelites with his passion for Turner, as he saw them representing two stages of artistic development; for having exhorted the young artist to study nature most carefully, 'rejecting nothing, selecting nothing, and scorning nothing', he goes on to say, 'then, when their memories are stored, and their imagination fed...let them take up the scarlet and gold, give reins to their fancy and show us what their heads are made of'[xiv]. It is into this second stage that Turner's work falls, and Goodwin himself from the mid 1870s, but most especially from around the turn of the century, more and more in his poetic use of colour and sensitive use of the pen, succumbed to the magical spell of Turner's work; so much so, that he subsequently observed that 'I wonder sometimes of the spirit of old Turner makes use of my personality! I often find myself doing the very things that he seemed to do'[xv]. Turner was important for Goodwin in two particular aspects of his work; in the first place, he was greatly influenced by Turner's skill in combining fact and fancy in his landscapes views, thus emulating that feature of Turner's work so aptly described by Ruskin as 'imaginative topography'; and secondly, he learned certain technical skills, such as the ability of achieving both breadth and detail in his water-colours, by a skilful and sensitive combination of wash and pen-work - characteristics that are well illustrated in much of his later work, especially from the years circa 1895-1925.

Like Turner, Goodwin was a master of all the techniques used in water-colour painting, employing at various times (and not infrequently all together) watercolour, bodycolour, pen and ink, chalk, pastel and gum, on white or tinted papers, with the whole sometimes neatly enclosed in a beautifully designed, hand-painted border. In order to achieve the subtle lighting effects associated with dawn and sunset - his favourite times of the day - he wiped and scraped and '...hammered at them with the blade of a safety-razor, a knife, sandpaper, sponge, rag, and a fitch brush!!! So many are the expedients that the despairing water-colour painter in the last has to resort to'[xvi].

Although Goodwin is now best remembered for his work in watercolours, he also worked from time to time in oils. His large oil painting of *Ali Baba and The Forty Thieves* was bought by the Tate Gallery under the terms of the Chantery Bequest of 300 guineas in 1901. [A smaller version of this painting is included in this catalogue, no 69.] Indeed, in the early part of his career, he seriously considered the possibility of working more extensively in oils. It may be that he was caught up in the prevailing belief that oil painting was a higher and more serious art form, and the one by which artistic reputations were made. Fortunately he sought the advice of Ruskin, who rightly observed that 'I have always felt deep regret at your taking to oil... The virtue of oil, as I understand it, is perfect delineation of solid form in deep local colour. It seems to me not only adverse to, but negative to [sic] partially, beautiful landscape effect...'[xvii]

Like Blake before him, Ruskin too sensed the limitations of the earthbound oil technique for the creation of poetic and imaginative landscape painting - an opinion shared by another critic who attacked some of Goodwin's exhibited oils as 'lacking the delicacy of his watercolour work'[xviii]. Moreover, Goodwin himself, although he continued to dabble in oils for the rest of his life, generally found the oil medium too intractable and unsuited to his artistic temperament, 'Washed, and put away brushes and oil paint, for a finish up of a week of - what is to me - a horrid material, after the purity of clean-smelling water-colour...'[xix].

In spite of his earlier Pre-Raphaelite training of working directly from nature, Goodwin, as his career progressed, worked more and more from memory. His normal procedure was to do sketches directly from nature and then work these sketches up in the studio, although it should be borne in mind that quite often the sketches were made some years before, as Goodwin noted in the catalogue of an exhibition he held at the Fine Art Society in 1896, when he wrote that 'though I date my pictures at the time of their completion. I would by no means have it inferred that the whole of the exhibition has been done within the last year. Some of the subjects were begun as many as twenty years ago'[xx].

Thus, although his work was firmly rooted in his own direct experiences, he increasingly recreated these experiences through the veil of his memory, as this allowed his imagination to raise a subject from being a 'mere portrait tied down to hard facts', into a poetic interpretation of his experience.

The importance of the role played by his memory and imagination, is seen more clearly when one notes from the titles of his numerous exhibited works, that Goodwin was an inveterate traveller, visiting not only all parts of Britain, but also Jersey, Holland, Italy, Switzerland, Egypt, Crete, Belgium, India, North America, the West Indies, New Zealand and Sicily. It could be argued that many of his best pictures were inspired by India and the 'gorgeous east', by Switzerland and the Alps - the experience of which prompted him, in his old age, to ask, 'Will there be anything more wonderful than the higher Alps in the Kingdom of Heaven?'[xxi]. And finally, of course, 'my own native land England always seems more than ever an epitome of all countries - the best of them "done in little"'[xxii].

Although the bulk of Goodwin's work could be correctly described as poeticised topography, he also had a penchant for imaginative works inspired by readings of the *Arabian Nights* (his grand-daughter recalls that *Sinbad* was one of his favourite stories), the Bible, Dante etc.

In addition to Turner and the Pre-Raphaelites, another source of inspiration for Goodwin's art was Oriental art, with which he well have come into contact as early as 1876 on his first visit to Egypt - although Oriental art was then becoming quite fashionable in European art circles. Certainly many of his compositions, framed as they often are by branches of trees or sprays of blossom, and sometimes with an emphasis on an asymmetrical design, suggest a knowledge of Oriental art. In fact, it is interesting to note in 1890 he shared an exhibition at the Fine Art Society with a show of Japanese art, and in the catalogue he observed that:

> Painted as some of them have been with the knowledge that Japanese art would be in the next room, there may have crept in unawares the hope that in landscape are the West should not play second fiddle to the East, though between Japanese and British painting

there can be no question of rivalry, the points of view of each being so utterly dissimilar. It seems quite questionable that the West takes knowledge, and is able to assimilate with advantage some of the colour and decorative design of the Eastern schools, but is a one sided business. The advantages are to us, and not to them, who seem to make shipwreck of their powers when they endeavour to engraft anything of ours into their own art... I am conscious of my own indebtedness both to Japanese and Moorish art...[xxiii]

Goodwin's delicate colour schemes, his finely felt sense of atmosphere, and his poetic treatment of landscape, have rightly made him one of the most distinctive and unique artists of his time; indeed, Goodwin's artistic vision is so highly personalised, that it would be difficult to confuse his work with any of his contemporaries. Nor should one forget that his career spans a remarkably long period, for although we tend to think of him as a Victorian, he was active as an artist until as late as 1932. Nevertheless, Goodwin's art was totally unaffected by the radical changes that took place in the art world in the first quarter of the twentieth century, and Cubism, Futurism, Expressionism, Dada and Surrealism, all left his own artistic vision quite intact. Of his contemporaries his own particular favourites were 'Arthur Rackham...Walter Crane and Kate Greenaway... and in his home,' recalls his grand-daughter, 'there were absolutely no "old masters"...and we were brought up knowing nothing at all about other great and famous artists. I think Turner was the only one I ever heard of till I went to school'[xxiv].

Although Goodwin stood aside from the mainstream of the twentieth century art, it is, somewhat ironically, precisely in the period after 1900 that much of his best work was produced, for it is encouraging to note that there is little evidence of any reduction in his artistic ability with advancing years. Indeed, much of his later work takes on an increasingly ethereal quality as his mastery of pen and wash, and of breadth and detail, so frequently achieve a quite magical unison.

His passion for painting was uncontrollable right to the end, and his grand-daughter recalls how in the 1920s, when he moved, with his daughters, into a new house with plain plastered walls, he

was made to promise to paint the walls - but one day the aunts went out on a shopping spree, and when they came back Grandpa had been unable to resist painting the walls of his little bedroom floor to ceiling in wavy red and yellow and black stripes with conventional sunflowers at the top of them. It was really very nice. He just couldn't help painting. He would get at lovely old bits of black oak furniture when people were out and paint them all over. Our house was full of furniture painted by Grandpa. Also he used to haunt the town rubbish tip, and collect bits of broken china which he made into the most lovely mosaics set in cement in iron blacksmith-made trays. These were set in the outside walls of the house and made into frames for mirrors and mantle-pieces etc. He used to employ a carpenter who made boxes and shelves etc. of plain deal which Grandpa then painted. I still have a 'play-box' with a wild cat in a lovely jungle painted by him...he seemed never to stop painting except to eat or bicycle or walk...[xxv]

i *Under the Hedge*, No. 156

ii FM Brown to James Leathart, 12 July 1864

iii *Spectator*, 8 December 1883

iv *Spectator*, 15 May 1886

v *Spectator*, 4 May 1889

vi The best public collection of Goodwin's work is to be found in Maidstone Museum and Art Gallery

vii *Notes on Prout and Hunt* in E T Cook and A Wedderburn (editors), *The Works of John Ruskin*, London: George Allen, 1903-1912, Volume 14

viii *Spectator*, 13 May 1879

ix *The Diary of Albert Goodwin*, privately published 1934. Entries on page 36, 18 July 1900 and page 22, Christmas 1888

x His grand-daughter recalls that he had masses of letters from Ruskin that were burnt by his daughters after his death. Letter to author 7 May 1978

xi Arthur Severn MSS, John Rylands Library, University of Manchester

xii *Spectator*, 1886

xiii *Diary*, page 37, 18 July 1900 and page 183, 1 June 1913

xiv Ruskin, *Works*, Volume 3, pages 623-24

xv *Diary*, page 133, 18 February 1911

xvi *Diary*, page 175, 17 March 1912

xvii Ruskin, *Works*, Volume 37, pages 212-13

xviii *Spectator*, 26 June 1880

xix *Diary*, page 132, 18 February 1911

xx *Imaginative Landscapes in Europe and Asia*, London: Fine Art Society, March 1896

xxi *Diary*, page 371, 1 December 1917

xxii *Imaginative Landscapes in Europe and Asia*, London: Fine Art Society, March 1896

xxiii *Collection of Watercolour Drawings of many-sided Nature by Albert Goodwin, RWS*, London: Fine Art Society, 1890

xxiv Letter to author, 7 May 1978

xxv loc cit

This essay is reprinted with editions from the article in the
Old Water-Colour Society's Club, Volume 54, 1979

BOGIE AND THE PROFESSOR

Thoughts on Ruskin and Goodwin

by David Wootton

John Ruskin's passion for contemporary art was quirky and parochial, but his taste for the modern painters of England was, at least initially, broad. While donning the persona of Turner's apologist, he also championed the younger Pre-Raphaelite Brotherhood. Through his association with the Pre-Raphaelites, he came to know both Arthur Hughes and Ford Madox Brown, and so met their pupil, Albert Goodwin, at the end of the 1860s. Ruskin was then an established, if controversial man of letters at the height of his powers, just embarking on a new career as Slade Professor of Fine Art at Oxford University. Goodwin was a shy, young, if brilliant, artist of lower-class background and Methodist persuasion. Despite, or possibly because of, this contrast, Ruskin immediately perceived Goodwin's qualities.

'Ruskin did me the honour', Goodwin wrote in 1909, 'soon after I knew him, to ask me to come and give him a lesson in water-colour painting. It was a flattering way of inviting me, and I went'. Himself a talented watercolourist, Ruskin would draw on the specific skills of young, professional artists to produce examples for his lectures and the classroom, and record, with increasing urgency, European buildings threatened with neglect or insensitive restoration. These artists were thus not only given the opportunity to learn from Ruskin, but to do so in the context of Continental travel.

By early in 1871, Ruskin had planned for Goodwin to accompany him on a trip to Switzerland and Italy, but this was postponed because of the Franco-Prussian War. As a result, Ruskin wrote to Goodwin on 19 March, asking him,

> to stay with me at a nice country inn about which I find the loveliest of subjects: but I can't paint them unless you are able to come...I will give you what price you think right for your drawings as fast as you can make them, and you will get used to me a little before we start for Verona

At Abingdon, Goodwin produced two views for the Rudimentary Series of the Ruskin Art Collection at Oxford. But Ruskin distinguished Goodwin from the more antiquarian of his disciples, and did not employ him as a copyist. In the Catalogue of a *Series of Drawings made for the St George's Guild* (1886), Ruskin later elucidated this distinction as one of kind rather than quality:

> I cannot guess whether in the association of these elaborately finished drawings with Mr Albert Goodwin's often literally flying memoranda, my Guild drawings will suffer from looking too literal, or Mr Goodwin's from looking too imaginative. But the same spirit of truth is in both.

However, he then enthused that,

> for pure aesthetic delight an untouched sketch of Albert Goodwin's on the spot is better than any finished drawing.

When Ruskin took Goodwin abroad, he expected him to produce work of imagination and delight but, more than that, Goodwin himself was almost literally enchanted. The furthest limit of his experience had then been Jersey (visited in 1864), and his conception of the world was permanently coloured by his tour with Ruskin, despite the extensive journeys he would later undertake far beyond Europe. 'When I first went to Italy', he wrote excitedly in his diary in 1909, 'it was my firm conviction that I should never be able to afford to go again, and here I am once more taking the family not only to Switzerland but Italy!'

After what might be called a dry run, to Matlock Spa, in June 1871, Ruskin and Goodwin departed for Italy on 13 April 1872. They were accompanied by Joan and Arthur Severn, who had also been present at Matlock, and by the wife and daughter of the Reverend J C Hilliard; Ruskin's servant, Crawley, was in attendance. The three month itinerary followed the general shape of the eighteenth-century Grand Tour. However, it was reorientated in order to refuse Rome the Augustan distinction of ultimate goal. Ruskin had never liked Rome, and from early on had thought its architecture 'heathenish'. The longest periods, of a fortnight each, were spent instead in the aesthetically and spiritually safer environments of Florence and Venice.

The trip was not a holiday; Ruskin would begin work at six almost every morning, preparing lectures, writing the monthly numbers of *Fors Clavigera* and correcting proofs of forthcoming books. Goodwin and Severn would thus have been the first to have heard, for example, the thoughts on early Italian art that went into *Val d'Arno*, the series of lectures he would later give at Oxford in 1873. The first of those lectures made a point concerning the continuity of European culture - from Ancient Greece to Mediaeval Italy and beyond - that Ruskin tried to convey to Goodwin. The imparting of such knowledge often took the form of sympathetic and encouraging dialogue, here instanced by one of Ruskin's less successful moments. As chronicled by Arthur Severn, Ruskin asked Goodwin for his impression of St Mark's, Venice:

> Goodwin looked a little shy, as we all knew him to be a singularly honest and straightforward man, we felt there was something he was afraid to tell out. The Professor, seeing it too, said, 'Don't mind my dear Albert, say whatever you like. Your opinion is sure to be worth having'. At last Goodwin said, 'Well Professor, if you really ask me and won't mind what I say, my first impression of the church and the domes above, and all the flags, was that it looked very like a travelling show'. The Professor burst out into a roar of laughter, in which we all joined. When he could speak, he said, 'Never mind Albert, I know perfectly well what you mean, but you will soon get to like it'

And if Goodwin failed to appreciate individual sights, he certainly succeeded in understanding the broader lessons of Ruskin's idiosyncratic interpretation of the Grand Tour.

At every turn in his later diary, Goodwin measured new geographical experiences against the distinct aesthetic developed in the company of Ruskin. For instance, during his first voyage through the West Indies in 1902, Goodwin gave a very Ruskinian gloss to Dr Johnson's belief that 'the object of travel is to visit the Shores of the Mediterranean':

> Certainly, though [Johnson] cared nothing for the pictorial, no land is so fair as that land I have looked on holding that is beautiful both of man's work and Nature's... Man's work here is vile, save in his sugar growing and cocoa cultivation... All that can be seen (save of the tropical foliage, and this is a very great exception) can be infinitely better seen in Switzerland and Italy, with all the added beauty of history and people. (28 February/15 March)

While Goodwin recognised the specifically painterly potential of tropical landscapes, he realised that the human dimension of such places was antithetical to Ruskin's Eurocentric reading of culture and religion.

More profoundly, though less perceptibly, Goodwin was affected by the language of Western thinking and feeling that underpinned Ruskin's teaching. Quoting Ruskin's response to a favourite landscape, that 'one has not *being* enough for it', he followed his master in retreating from direct engagement with his environment to recollection of it. On his journey to India in 1917, he wrote:

> How much more pleasant though Benares is in retrospection...To me this method of work is one of the happy things of the Art I practise, for I get the realization of a place twice over, and often *the memory makes the scene a better one than the first experience.* (1 December)

Only by distancing themselves from an object of concern were Ruskin and Goodwin able to reconcile themselves to the power of landscape. Wordsworthians to a degree, they would both have applauded the potent advice of the Romantic poet to recollect 'emotion in tranquility'.

Goodwin had set out to establish himself as a Romantic evangelist who, through painting, would unlock the sealed book of nature and reveal the spiritual world:

> The whole natural world down to the smallest detail, is one great allegory, typically of the spiritual world... Beauty - the Beauty that is in the landscape - is a sealed book to many, hence in a degree the landscape painter may magnify his calling. (Christmas 1888)

At the same time, he still insisted on his own humility, and always attempted a balance, or compromise between the dogmatic positions of others, and even between the elements of painting.

This role of visual interpreter, and the tempering compromise that decided the look of his interpretations, both derived from Ruskin. The early Ruskin, in particular, was fond of parallelling The Bible and the Book of Nature. And Goodwin praised Ruskin in his diary for, 'ballyragging...me into love of form when I was getting too content with colour alone.' Following Ruskin's advice, Goodwin would 'magnify his calling' by attending as much to line and form as to colour, and by generally balancing the elements of painting. Yet in order to develop a position of such confidence and independence, Goodwin found it necessary to censure Ruskin's own excessive love and use of colour.

Goodwin blamed his own artistic failings on the emphasis that had been placed by Ruskin and the Pre-Raphaelites on the use of bright colour. Overcoming any guilt he felt at criticising Ruskin, he wrote with condescension that the older man had 'loved with the love of a child bright colour', as if he were ignorant, or innocent, of visual reality. He even implied that Ruskin suffered from delusions:

> [Ruskin's] marble pillars that he painted of St Mark's, I used to look at in wonder! I think he *thought* he saw the colour he put on; but to me the actual reticence would have been far more subtle and beautiful. (1 December 1918)

Inevitably for a late Victorian landscapist such as Goodwin, reticence and subtlety suggest the work of Whistler as a contrast to that of Ruskin, as a result of their legal case in 1878:

> Ruskin's strong point was never colour. He was a safe guide in all matters of form or sentiment, but as to any interest in tone-values or greys, 'he cared for none of these things'... it was this feeling that made him look at Whistler's work with the contempt he did, and doubtless prompted the criticism which led to the law suit for libel that Whistler brought against him... Neither of these two schools could appreciate or understand eachother. There's the pity of it, and both sides lack the charity that thinketh no evil.

Goodwin praised Whistler's use of colour as restrained and economical, suggesting that, in the act of painting, a positive emphasis had been placed on other, perhaps more formal, considerations. And in purely aesthetic terms, Whistler's palette appealed to Goodwin. 'Turner's favourite colour was yellow', Goodwin wrote on 9 January 1912. 'It's curious, of the three it's the one I care *least* for'. Whistler, too, cared little for yellow, for he could more easily integrate red and blue into his extensive use of tonal greys.

However, Goodwin eventually chose loyalty to Ruskin over his attraction to Whistler, because Ruskin's interests were less self-centred:

> The plane on which Ruskin stood was immeasurably higher than the other and in its way the upward. Whistler's tended downward. Ruskin with all his seeming arrogance in his writing was in Art and in feeling humility itself, while Whistler's thought was mostly, see how dextrous I am, who can do it like this? And with that thought taking lead always the man's way is the way of deterioration. The vale of humility is the only safe place in Art as in life. 'He that is down need fear no fall'.

Goodwin praised Whistler's use of colour as reticent and economical, but also as subtle. To a mind as Bible-soaked as that of Goodwin, 'subtle' was an epithet descriptive of the serpent, the origin of sin. 'He that is down need fear no fall' indeed! Behind Ruskin was that 'horrible German spirit' embodied in Britain by Carlyle, but behind Whistler was Oscar Wilde, and Goodwin despised Wilde as a degenerate. If the mature Goodwin failed to appreicate Ruskin's strictly visual judgment , he continued to value his introduction to a wider world charged with moral meaning.

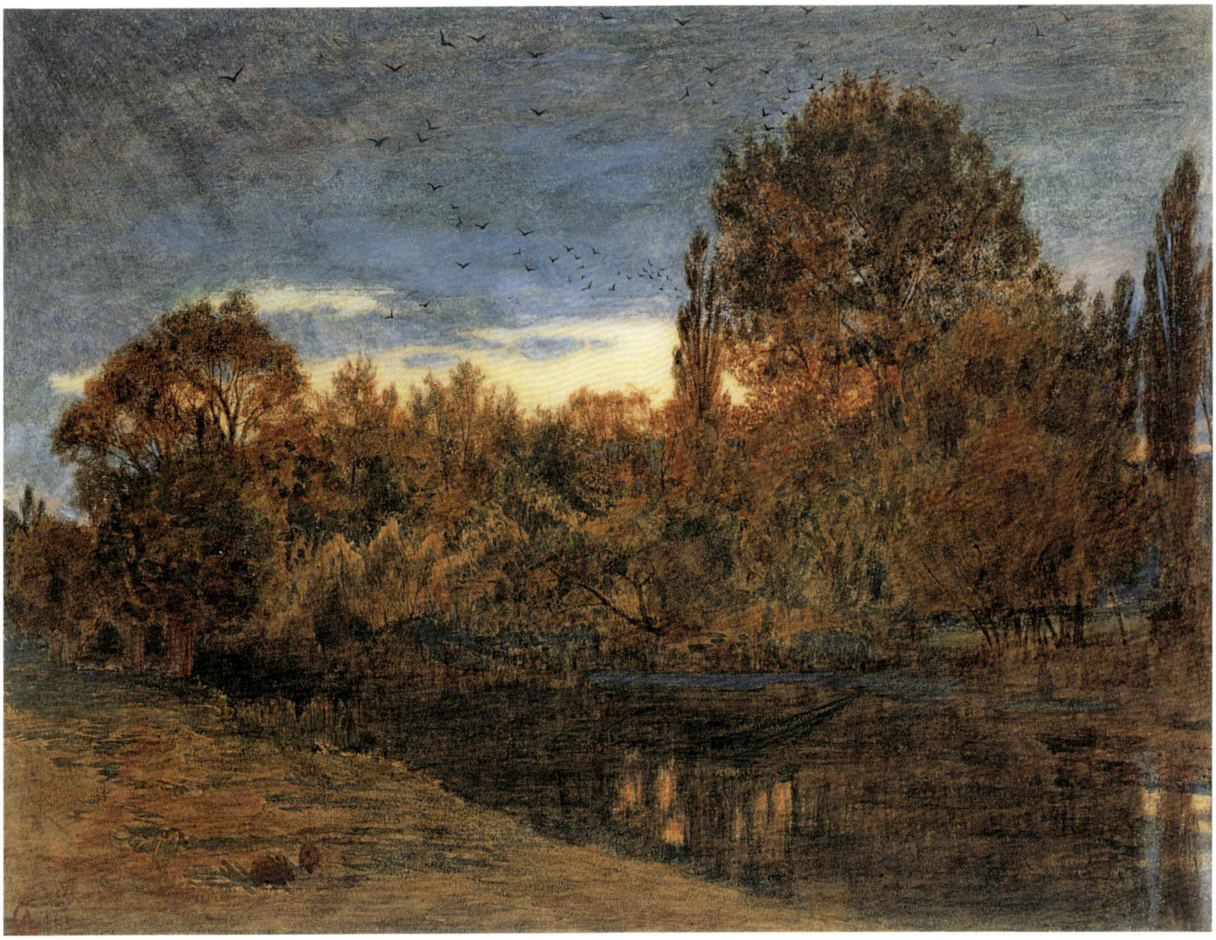

1 SUNSET THROUGH WOODLAND

signed with monogram and dated 65
watercolour with bodycolour
13 ½ x 18 ¾ INCHES

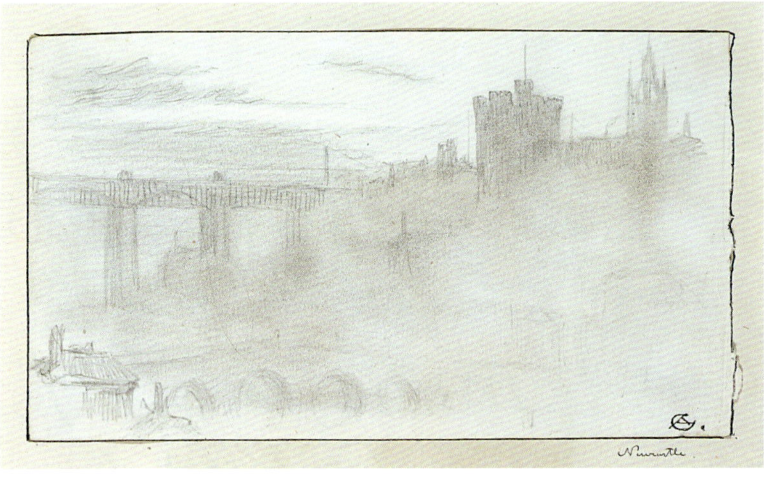

2 NEWCASTLE

signed with monogram and inscribed with title below mount
pencil
3 ½ x 6 ¼ INCHES

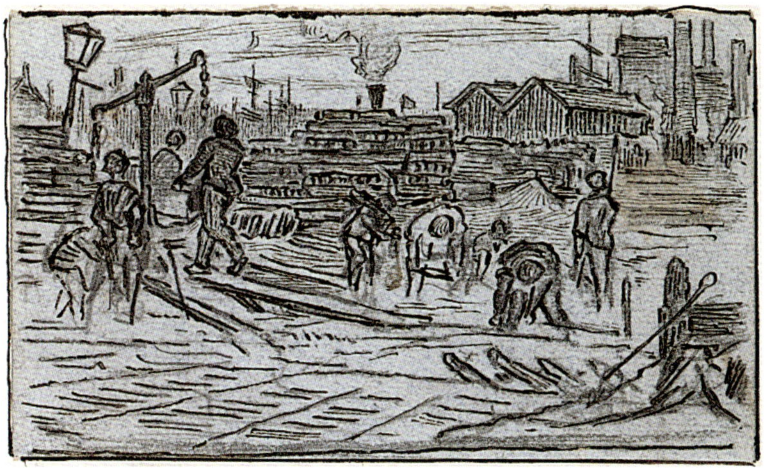

3 THE DOCKS
pen and ink and pencil on tinted paper
3 x 5 INCHES

4 STUDIES OF FARM ANIMALS
signed with initials
and dated 'May 30th/71'
watercolour and pencil
6 ¾ x 5 INCHES

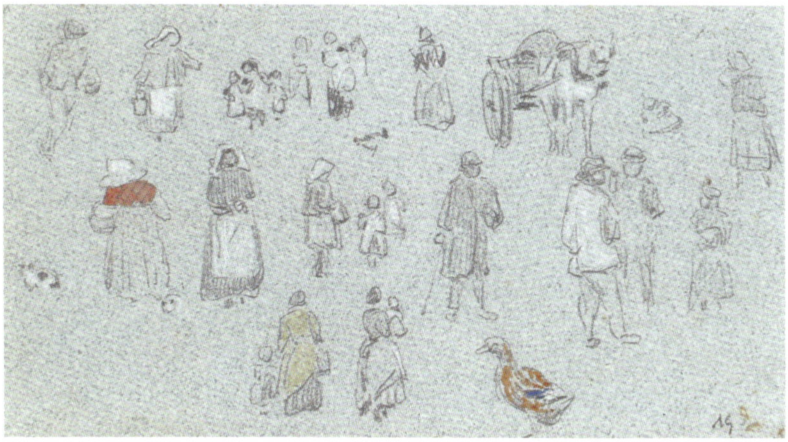

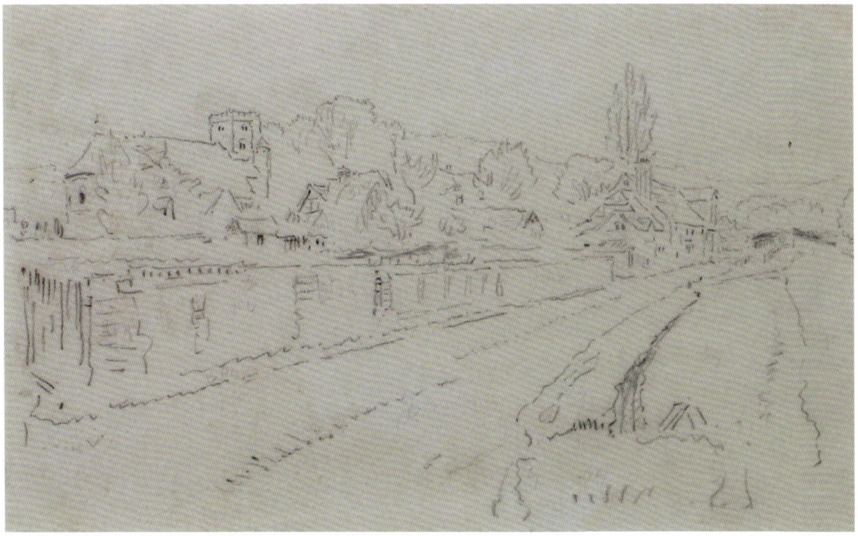

5 THE VILLAGE STREET
pencil on tinted paper
6 ¼ x 10 ¼ INCHES

A SKETCHBOOK OF 1872

The Tour with John Ruskin

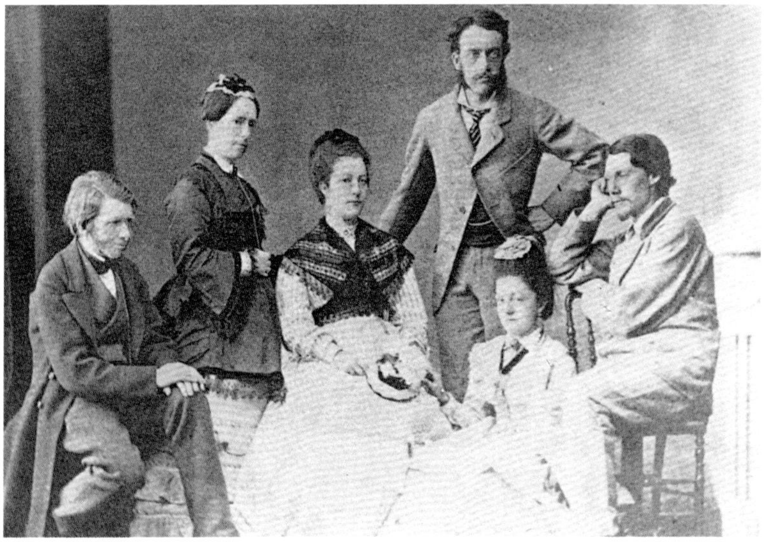

Albert Goodwin with John Ruskin in Italy in 1872

left to right:
John Ruskin, Mrs J C Hilliard, Mrs Joan Severn, Arthur Severn, Constance Hilliard, Albert Goodwin

In 1872, Albert Goodwin, among others, accompanied John Ruskin on a tour of Switzerland and Italy. For Goodwin, it was a seminal experience, perhaps the seminal experience of his career. Not only was it his first ever taste of foreign travel, but it was taken in the company of a writer expert in the subject of landscape painting. Seeing Europe with Ruskin helped him to define himself in terms of the critic's aesthetic, and so synthesise its Turnerian and Pre-Raphaelite elements in his own practice.

A knowledge of the tour, and of its affect on Goodwin, can now be further illumined by a sketchbook of drawings that the artist produced en route. The sketchbook drawings add helpful details to an understanding of both Goodwin's appreciation of the itinerary, and of the development of his working methods. This brief text rehearses that itinerary, giving a context for the sketches and so suggesting their importance both to the art of Goodwin and to a study of Ruskin.

The tour of 1872 was for Ruskin one in a series in which he examined the art and landscape so central to his writing, and also revived and reviewed feelings concerning his cultural and personal experience; for he first went abroad in 1825, at the age of six, and first visited Italy and Switzerland in 1832, at the age of thirteen. Most of the places that he and his party visited

continued on page 26

Place names in **bold** *refer to the most important destinations visited by Ruskin and his party.*

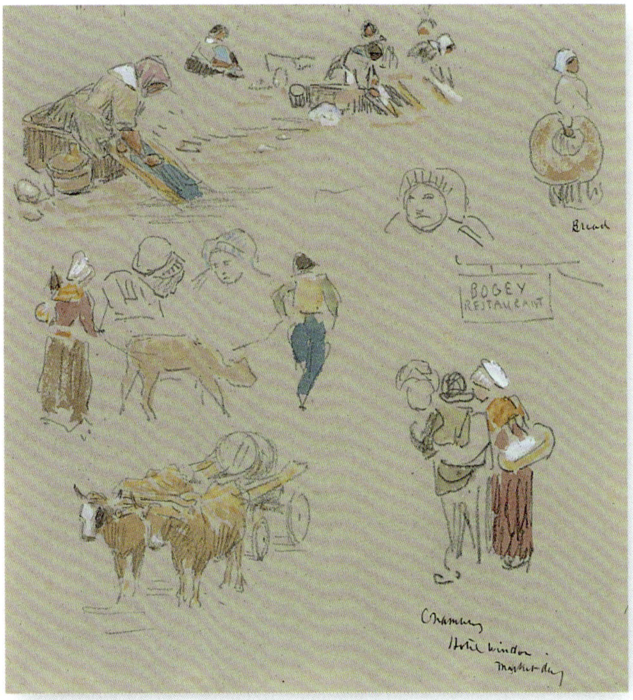

6 CHAMBERY, HOTEL WINDOW, MARKET DAY

inscribed with title

pencil and watercolour

6 ½ x 6 INCHES

Albert Goodwin did not begin to keep a diary until 1883, and his experiences of the trip can only be appreciated indirectly, through his drawings and through the writings of others, including Arthur Severn's posthumously published memoir of John Ruskin. Severn described an incident concerning himself which may have taken place while Goodwin was next door working on this drawing:

At Chambéry I was busy making a sketch on the balcony outside our sitting-room, leaving my wife on the sofa reading a book. After an hour or so I turned into the room and found her in floods of tears. She said: 'Oh I don't mind, it's nothing. I'm reading Misunderstood. It will be all right'. However, it wasn't all right for the waiter came in at that moment to lay luncheon, and I, fearing he might think we had been quarrelling, had to explain in my bad French that my wife was reading a very sad book – 'un livre trés malheureux –; he smiled and seemed to understand the situation but I have never felt quite certain in my own mind whether he did or not.

(James Dearden (editor), *The Professor. Arthur Severn's Memoir of John Ruskin*, London: George Allen & Unwin, 1967, page 52)

in 1872 had long been known and valued by him; he returned to them precisely because he wished to further explore their cultural riches, and explain them to others, both his companions on the tour, and his audiences and readers. Recently appointed as the first Slade Professor of Fine Art at Oxford, he had need to prepare lectures on his chosen subject of the early Italian Renaissance. In order to deepen his knowledge, he would, in particular, examine the work of Botticelli against that of Michelangelo in the Sistine Chapel, Rome, and make his first visit to Assisi.

At the same time, Ruskin had reasons to be away from England, and in sympathetic, supportive company. He had recently vacated one of his two family homes, that on Denmark Hill, and had not properly settled into Brantwood, his new property on Lake Coniston, in the Lake District. But far more emotionally disturbing was his relationship with, and love for, Rose La Touche, a hyper-anxious evangelical Irishwoman thirty years his junior. The silence that followed his proposal of marriage in 1866 had led to his breakdown in 1871, and continued to torture him; her attempt to revive contact with him, while he was in Venice, would bring his tour of 1872 to an abrupt end. And there was a backdrop to this emotional torment, provided by the aftermath of European war: the devastation of Paris and the unification and modernisation of Italy emphasised the frailty of the civilisation that Ruskin found so nurturing.

Ruskin financed, organised and aimed to control his tours of Europe. He chose his companions carefully, from among those who would provide him with comfort, and those whom he could help. His cousin, Joan Agnew, fitted both criteria. As he had once been her guardian, so she rapidly became his, her recent marriage to the painter Arthur Severn marking an outward maturity and independence. But she continued to depend on him for financial security, and it was he who enabled her to travel to Rome with her husband to meet her father-in-law, Joseph Severn. His relationships with the others on the tour, including Goodwin, were less fraught with complication. Mrs Kate Hilliard and her daughter Constance were close and reliable friends; Frederick Crawley a most trusted servant.

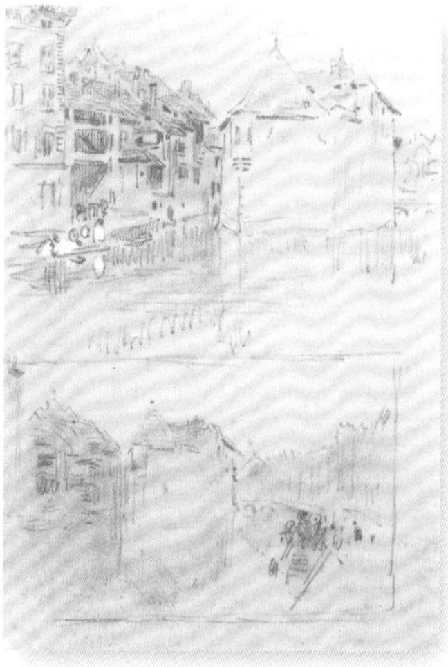

7 ANNECY

inscribed 'Annecy. Prison. clear water / washerwomen... /... children - Soldiers, old houses - water...'

pencil and bodycolour on tinted paper

9 x 6 INCHES

drawing of a view through an arch with figures in pencil and bodycolour on reverse

Ruskin's party left London on Friday 12 April; it probably travelled mostly by rail, via Dover, Calais and **Paris** (13 April), then down the Rhone Valley to **Geneva** (14 April). Ruskin had many fond memories of Geneva, especially as a centre for his impressive studies of geology and meteorology. These he had used to help himself understand and explain Turnerian topography, and now revived to encourage Goodwin. He noted in his diary (15 April) that 'Goodwin and Arthur [were] hard at work on my well

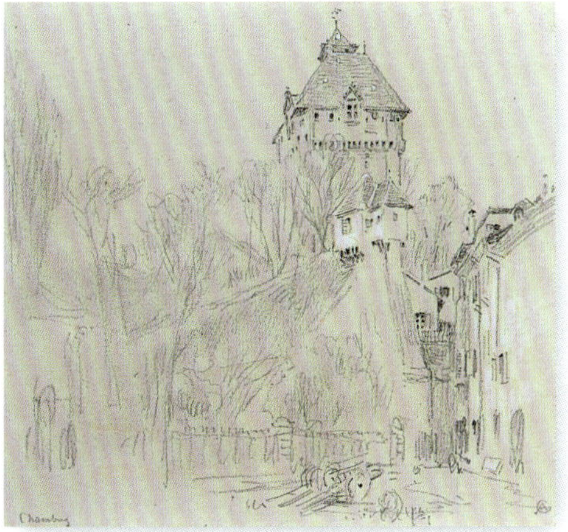

8 CHAMBERY

signed with monogram and inscribed with title
pencil with bodycolour
5 ¼ x 6 INCHES

9 MONTE ROSA VINEYARDS

inscribed with title
pencil with bodycolour and pen and ink
6 x 9 INCHES

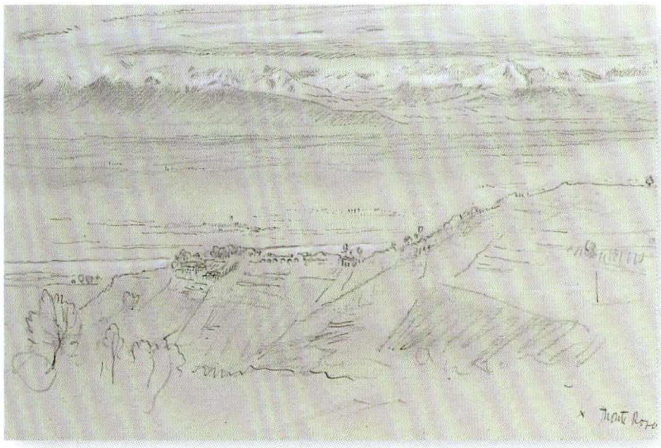

known path, at the sunset over Bonneville'; Severn later remembered that Ruskin had been 'anxious to take us for a drive up the Salève to get a view of Mont Blanc in the evening sunlight. The expedition was a great success: Mont Blanc behaved beautifully...Goodwin and I did sketches on the spot.' However, the sketches from the book that are illustrated here were made by Goodwin at the following destinations, **Annecy** (16 April) and **Chambéry** (19 April). While Ruskin corrected the proofs of *Elementary Drawing*, his forthcoming manual, Goodwin worked independently on his elemental drawings. Though Severn remembered Ruskin 'in the best of spirits', Ruskin himself had noted the 'dismal inn, and more dismal morning' at Chambéry (20 April).

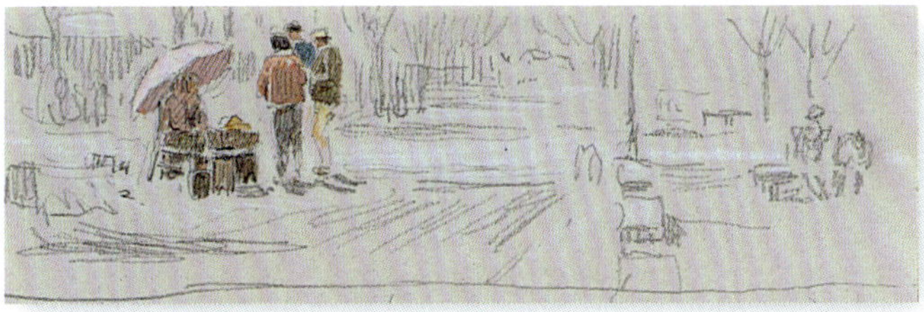

10 CARRARA MOUNTAINS, SPEZZIA: MARBLE SHINING LIKE SNOW (detail)

inscribed with title and dated '26th April'
watercolour and pencil with bodycolour
6 x 9 INCHES
drawing of an ox cart in pencil and bodycolour on reverse

According to Ruskin it remained 'wet all the way to **Turin**' (20 April) and, though the skies brightened temporarily, a 'storm [broke] among Apennine to **Genoa**' (22 April), where 'dismal rain' continued to fall (23 April). Apart from a visit to the monastery of Superga, outside Turin (21 April), Ruskin and his party probably spent most time surveying the palace picture galleries; these included the Galleria Sabada, in Turin, where, in 1858, Ruskin had, in studying Veronese's *Solomon and Sheba*, undergone what he later described as his 'unconversion', an important shift in his belief from evangelicalism to a religion of humanity. Leaving Turin, they travelled along the coast to stay at **Sestri Levante** (23 April), the beauty of which only Ruskin appreciated; according to Severn, the others 'all rather rebelled. It was very hot; the

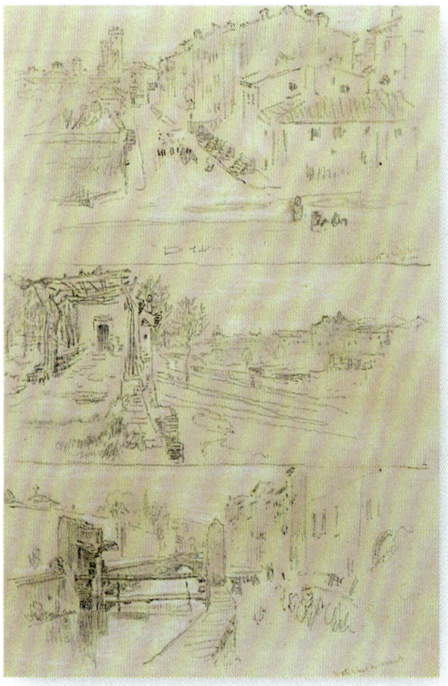

11 WATER WHEEL

inscribed indistinctly with title and other notes

pencil with pen and ink and bodycolour

8 ¾ x 5 ¾ INCHES

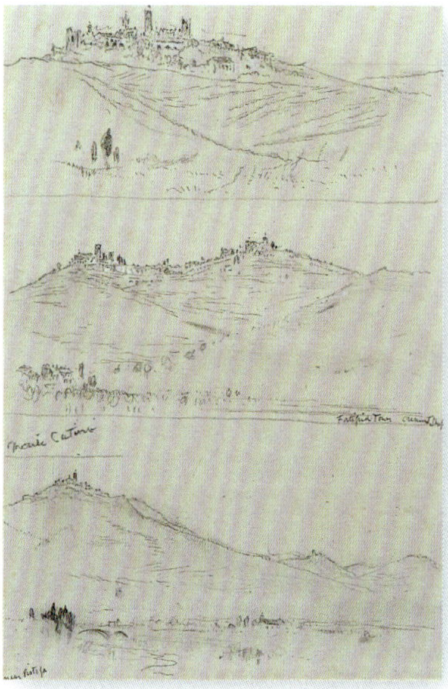

12 ITALIAN FORTIFIED TOWNS

inscribed 'Fortified Town. Crescent Shaped / Monte Catini Pistoia'

pencil with pen and ink and bodycolour

9 x 6 INCHES

windows of the hotel were not properly shut...; our sitting room was full of flies; the beach was dirty'. So they quickly moved on to **La Spezia**, arriving in moonlight (24 April), and next day exploring the valley and visiting an Italian warship (25 April). On leaving La Spezia for Pisa, Goodwin drew the Carrara Mountains, with their famous marble quarries, the material source for so many of the sculptures that Ruskin admired.

Ruskin had intended **Pisa** to be one of the more important stops on the journey, an exemplar of late mediaeval culture. On the first full day in the city (27 April), Ruskin took the party across the River Arno from the Hotel Victoria to look at Santa Maria della Spina, an exquisite chapel of the thirteenth and fourteenth centuries (built to house the sacred relic of a fragment of Christ's crown of thorns). However, he received his first great disappointment on finding that it was in the radical process of being demolished prior to rebuilding and restoration. This experience would be repeated a few days later, when, on visiting **Lucca** (30 April-3 May), he discovered that Santa Maria della Rosa, to him the sister chapel to that in Pisa, was also under threat. In Pisa, he compensated by spending many hours making drawings, sometimes in the company of Goodwin and Severn, and sometimes alone; his records of such favourite buildings as the Palazzi Gambacorti and Guinigi, the Duomo and the Campo Santo, as well as the chapel itself, would be integrated into the Oxford lectures collected as *Val d'Arno*. In Lucca, he wrote prefaces to *Christian Art and Symbolism* by the Reverend St John Tyrwhitt and to his own lecture on Michelangelo and Tintoretto, as well as passages of *Fors Clavigera*, a long series of wilful, urgent, even prophetic public letters. When the party left Pisa for **Florence** (8 May), Goodwin sketched the fortified towns en route and the Ponte Vecchio on arrival. Followed by rain and wind, the party stayed only briefly at this stage in the Tuscan capital; however, Ruskin did find time to visit the Duomo and Santa Maria Novella, and probably the major galleries.

As the party moved south from Florence (11 May) to **Rome** (12 May), Ruskin became increasingly irritable, his mood not helped by the continuing rain. Joan Severn wrote to Ruskin's friend, Charles Eliot Norton, the Harvard academic, that Ruskin was 'much out of humour, with everything, or, rather, triumphant at having his bad opinion of things in Rome confirmed'. Goodwin, however, obviously felt a great sense of expectation, as suggested by the drawings he made on arriving in the Roman Campagna, first of Narni and then of a distant view of Rome itself. Even Ruskin accepted that the city had much to offer, as he settled into one of his more concentrated periods of work. Over a stretch of ten days, he studied the work of Botticelli in the Sistine Chapel, to the detriment of Michelangelo, for his forthcoming Oxford lectures, *Ariadne Florentina*; he also visited the surviving Romanesque churches. As a result, the other members of the party were mostly left to their own devices. Joan and Arthur spent time with Joseph Severn, in his apartment overlooking the Fontana di Trevi, while Goodwin drew many of the city's most memorable sights, including the Colosseum, the Roman Forum, the Teatro Marcellus and the Piazza Barberini. As always, Ruskin was attentive to changes in the weather and the effect that it had on him; so he noted in his diary, 'glowing sunshine with painted sky' (17 May), 'soft grey sky; flaky cloud' (18 May) and 'fierce dust and sirocco, making me ill' (19 May).

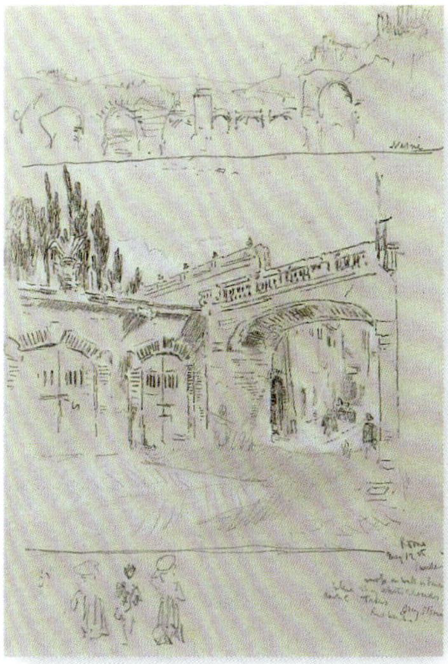

13 NARNI; ROME
inscribed with title and colour notes and dated 'Sunday May 12th'
pen and ink and pencil with bodycolour
9 x 6 INCHES
drawing of a landscape in pencil and bodycolour on reverse

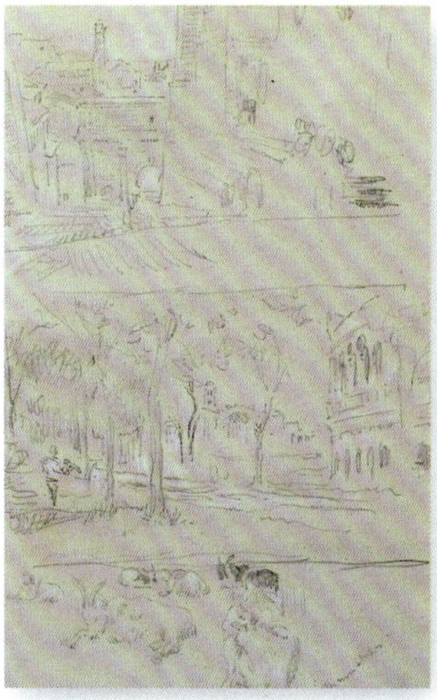

14 THE ROMAN FORUM
inscribed 'The Seven Sisters'
pencil with pen and ink and bodycolour
9 x 6 INCHES
drawings of goats and other figures in pencil and bodycolour on reverse

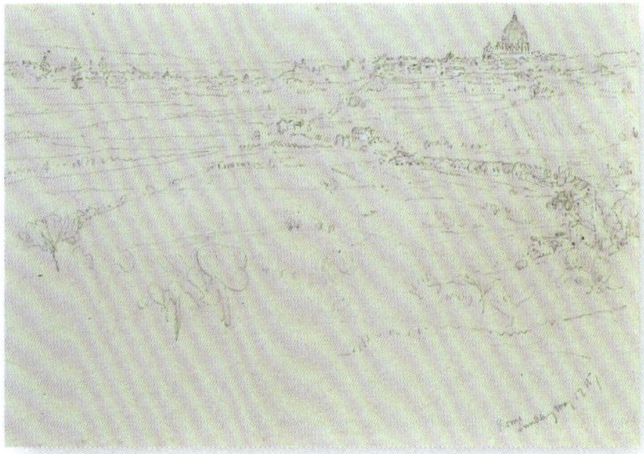

15 A DISTANT VIEW OF ROME
inscribed 'Rome' and dated 'Sunday May 12th'
pencil with bodycolour
6 x 9 INCHES

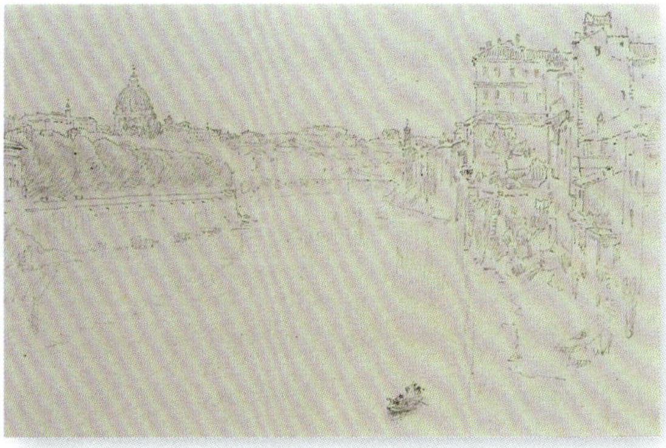

16 THE TIBER WITH ST PETER'S, ROME
pencil with bodycolour
6 x 9 INCHES

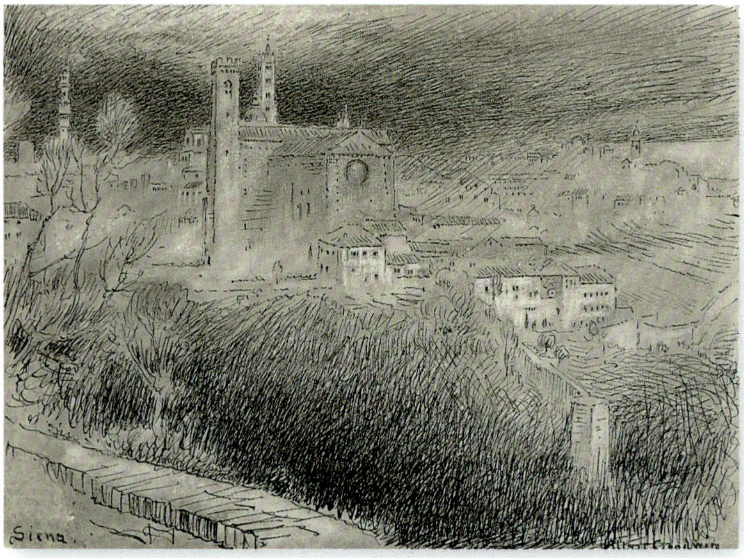

17 SIENA
signed and inscribed with title
pen and ink and monochrome watercolour with bodycolour
6 x 9 ½ INCHES

Ruskin gradually improved in health and temperament as the party moved north again, leaving Rome for **Assisi** (21 May). Even Ruskin was visiting the city for the first time, and Severn remembered that they 'liked it better than any of the other places. It was quiet and we were not pestered by beggars. Goodwin did some beautiful pencil sketches here and the Professor gave him the very highest praise'. The subjects of these sketches certainly included the famous monastery, and especially 'the Fathers of all the flying buttresses', as Ruskin described them to Goodwin. The party went from Assisi to **Perugia** for a day (24 May), the excursion enabling Ruskin to properly appreciate the merits of Perugino. Then, on leaving Assisi, it travelled via Florence (25 May) and **Siena** (27 May) to **Orvieto** (30 May). There Goodwin visited the market in the company of Ruskin, who recalled the event two years later, in writing the lecture 'Giotto's Pet Puppy'; considering the warm red ochre of the earth of the Apennines, he described the 'steps of its cathedral occupied on market-day with such a company of lively modern Etruscan pots'. Once again in **Florence** (1 June), and for a more substantial stay, Ruskin set to work, devoting attention mainly to the Baptistery, and leaving Goodwin to make sketches, including studies of the Via Crucis.

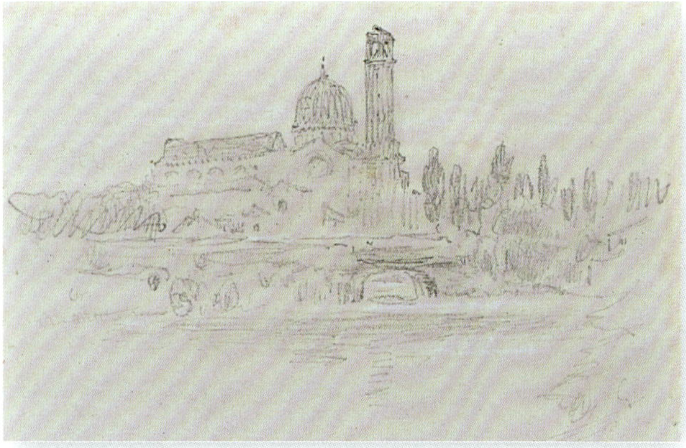

18 PADUA (detail)
inscribed with title and colour notes and dated 'June 15th'
pencil with bodycolour
9 x 6 INCHES

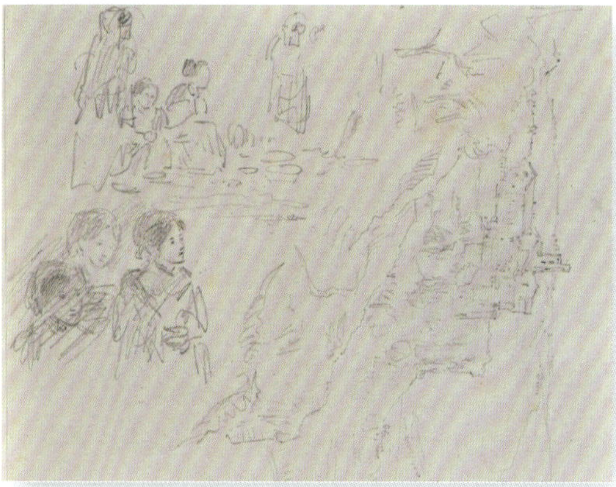

19 ORVIETO
inscribed with title and dated 'May 30th /72'
pencil
6 x 9 INCHES
includes sketches of Italian peasant women

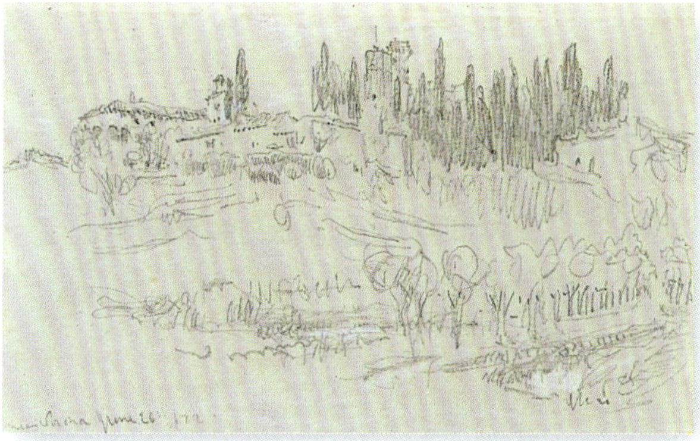

20 NEAR VERONA I
inscribed with title and dated 'June 20th /72'
pencil with pen and ink and bodycolour
9 x 6 INCHES

21 NEAR VERONA II
inscribed 'Verona' and with colour notes and dated 'June 21st'
pencil with bodycolour
6 x 9 INCHES

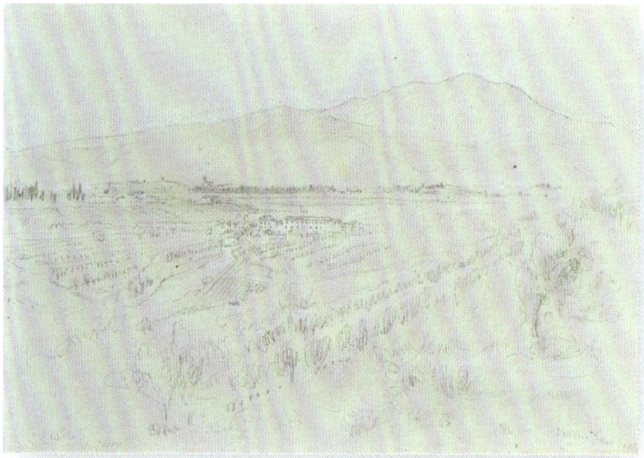

22 LAGO DI GARDA
inscribed with title and colour notes and dated 'June 16th /72'
pencil with bodycolour
6 x 9 INCHES
drawing of trees in pencil and bodycolour on reverse

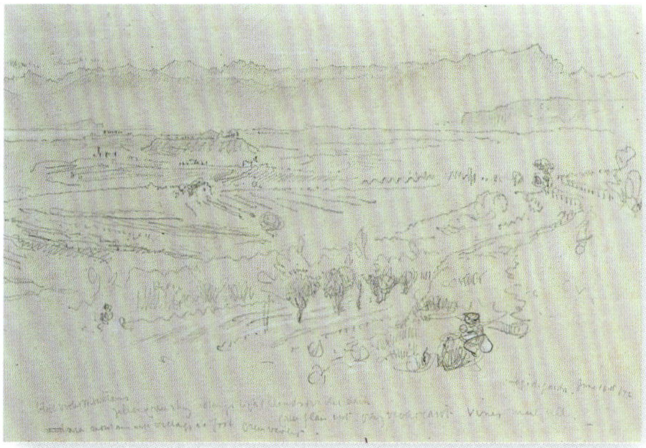

The final stage of the party's journey through Italy augured well; for though Ruskin noted at **Bologna** (14 June) of a 'pain in side (bilious)', the weather was 'perfectly fine...and very hot'. Verona and Venice, two of the most important sites in Ruskinian topography, were surely expected to prove the climaxes of the trip. Goodwin made a sketch of Padua on the way to **Verona** (15 June), and continued to concentrate on drawing, both the city and surroundings, while Ruskin prepared a pamphlet for the Arundel Society on the Cavalli tombs in Santa Anastasia. On arrival in **Venice** (2 July), the party was greeted by Rawdon Brown, as expert as his old friend Ruskin in the history and culture of the city. Ruskin encouraged the party to enthuse about its major sights, though was amused that Goodwin should liken the Byzantine splendour of San Marco to a 'travelling show'. Then, when Ruskin turned to his studies, examining the work of Carpaccio at the Scuola di San Giorgio degli Schiavoni, Goodwin again made many drawings, concentrating on such picturesque elements as the traditional fishing boats. Goodwin's work was admired by John Wharlton Bunney, another of Ruskin's protégés, best known for his depiction of the facade of San Marco. He remembered how on one evening 'I went to see Mr Goodwin's sketches; he has a good many. I was greatly pleased with them. Some of them are very lovely, very tender and beautiful'. He described Goodwin himself as 'quiet, practical, full of feeling. No gush but very earnest, without pretension of any kind'.

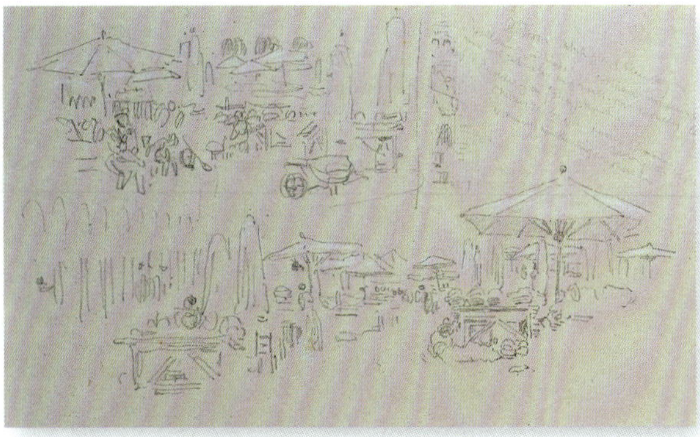

23 VENETIAN MARKET

inscribed 'Afternoon with grey & blue sky. Swallows...costume nondescript...crockery in foreground...cabbages, onions & lemons with yellow baskets...' and 'Venice' and dated 'June 72' on reverse

pencil with bodycolour

6 x 9 INCHES

drawings of Venice in pencil and bodycolour on reverse

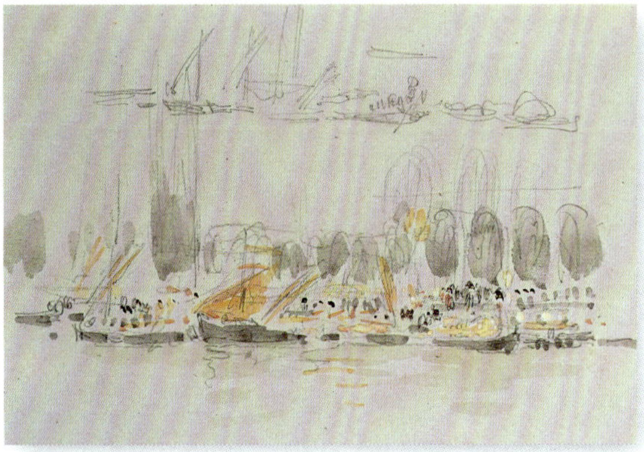

24 QUAYSIDE, VENICE

watercolour and pencil with bodycolour

6 x 9 INCHES

drawing of Venetian fishing boats in watercolour and pencil on reverse

Unfortunately, Goodwin's experience of Venice was soon brought to an end. Ruskin learned from the writer George MacDonald that Rose la Touche was anxious to see him. At first unwilling to interrupt his work, or again subject himself to the pain of rejection, he sent a telegram (30 June) and letters (5 July); but he soon decided to return home. Goodwin, Crawley and the Hilliards went with him, while the Severns travelled separately. The speed at which he and his companions crossed the continent indicates his sense of urgency, and he could no longer allow Goodwin much time for drawing. The route taken, in late July, was as follows: **Milan** (13), **Como** (14), **Baveno** (15), **Domo d'Ossola** (19), **Simplon** (20), Brieg, **Sion** (23), **Geneva** (24), Sens, Paris, Herne Hill (26).

For Ruskin, this journey marked the beginning of the end of his relationship with Rose La Touche, for she would die in 1875. But for Goodwin it marked the end of the beginning of his life as a landscape painter and traveller. 'When I first went to Italy', he wrote excitedly in his diary thirty-five years later, on 21 April 1909, 'it was my firm conviction that I should never be able to afford to go again, and here I am taking once more the family not only to Switzerland but Italy!' The tour of 1872 may have represented for Ruskin a personal failure. However, he should have considered it a success, if only in its essential contribution to making an artist of Goodwin.

David Wootton

Numbers 6-24 (excluding no 17) are all pages from a sketchbook taken on the 1872 tour with Ruskin.

25 RYE AND WINCHELSEA
signed and dated 73
watercolour
5 x 6 ¾ INCHES

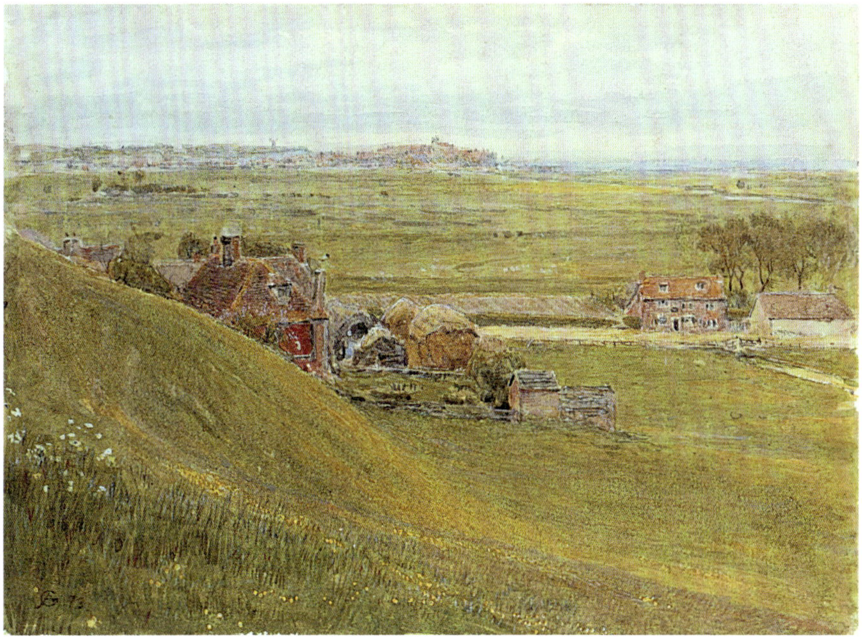

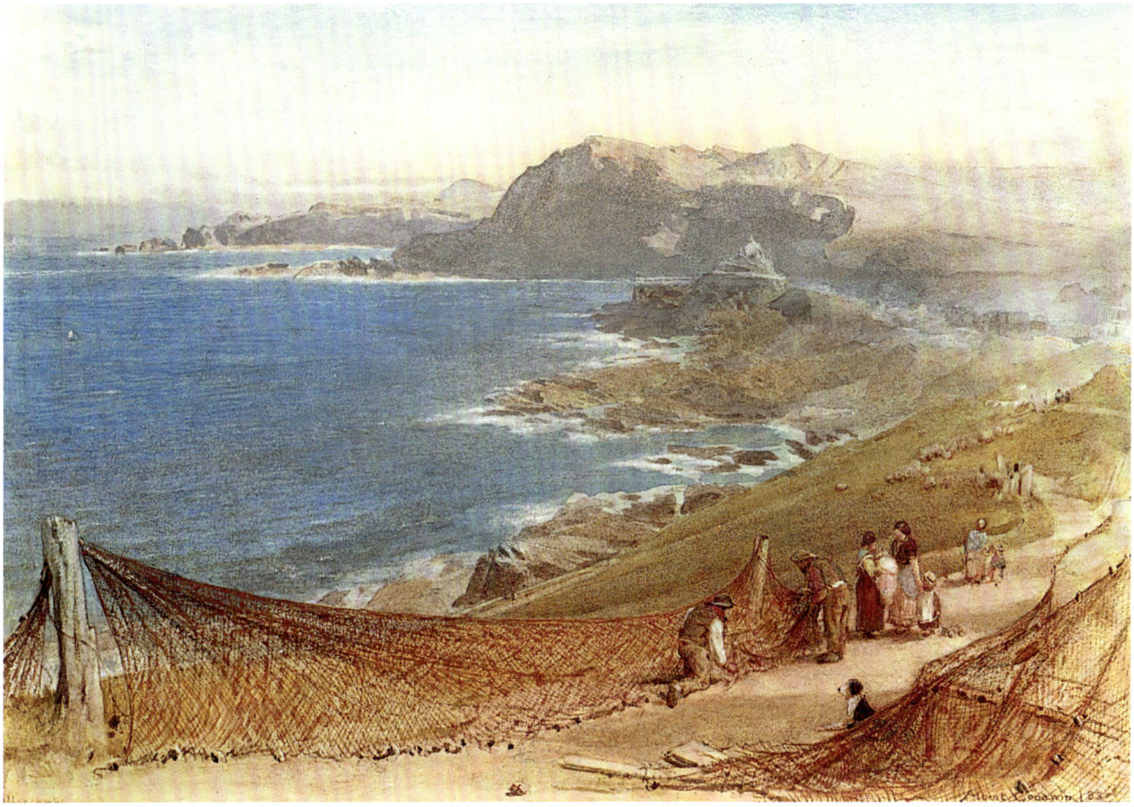

26 CLEANING NETS, ILFRACOMBE
signed, inscribed 'Ilfracombe' and dated /83
watercolour
9 ½ x 13 ½ INCHES

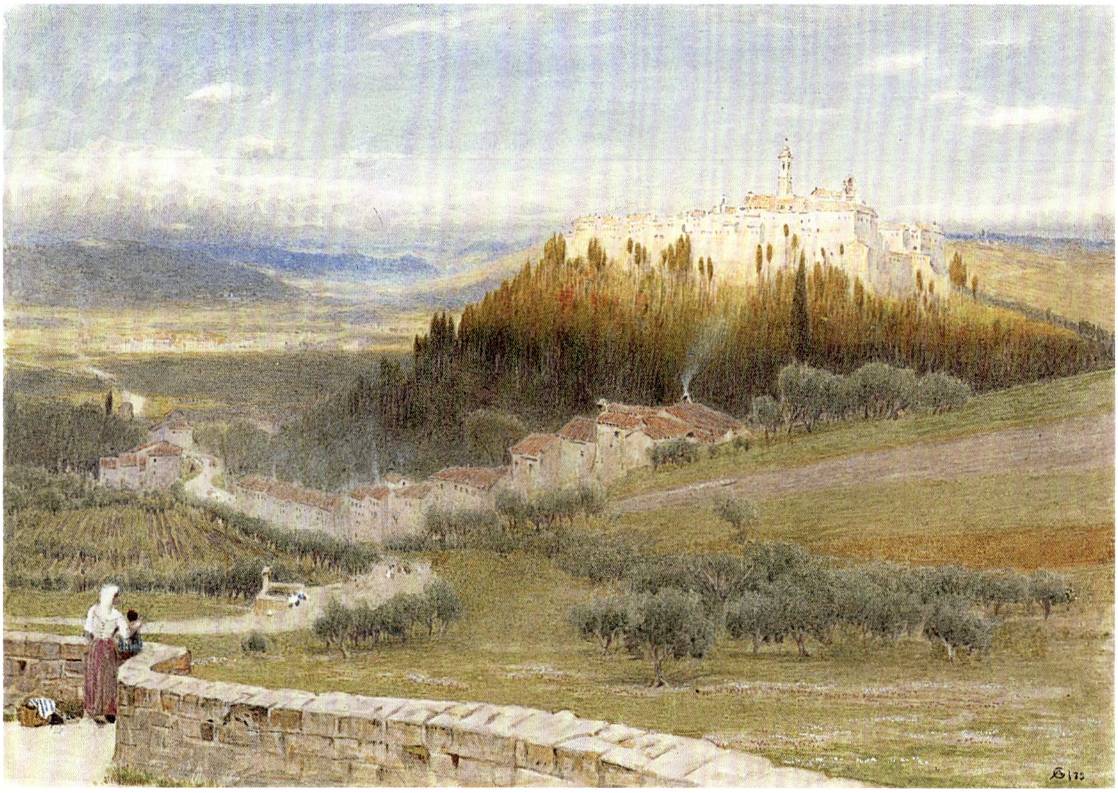

27 CERTOSA

signed with monogram and dated 73
watercolour and bodycolour
9 x 13 ½ INCHES

EXHIBITED: 'An Exhibition of Watercolours by Albert Goodwin', Southgate Gallery, Shifnal, May 1982, No 3

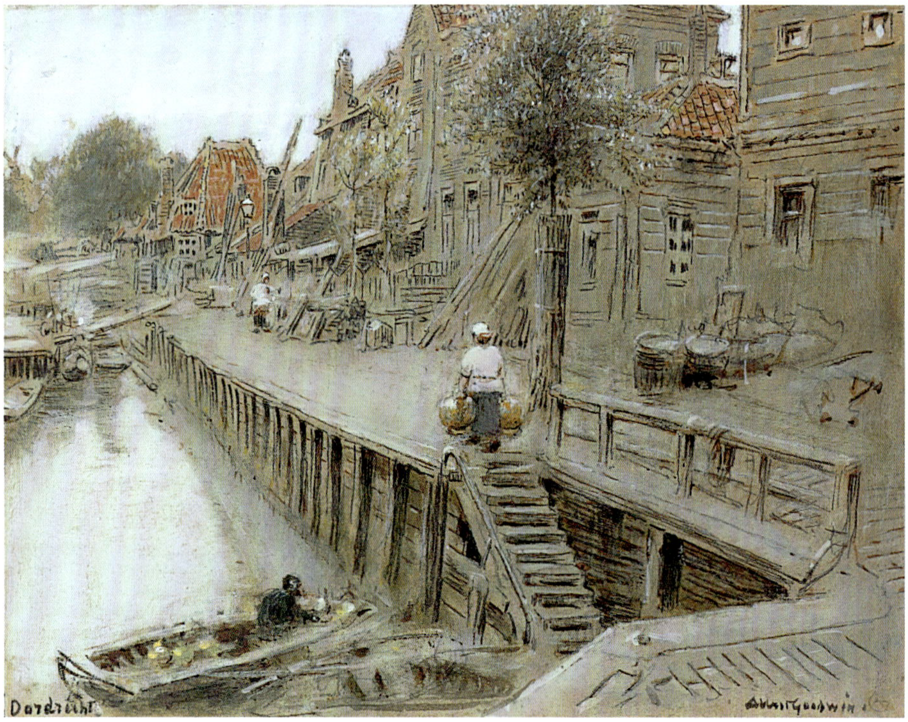

28 DORDRECHT

signed with monogram, signed and inscribed with title
watercolour with bodycolour and pen and ink
9 ¼ x 12 INCHES

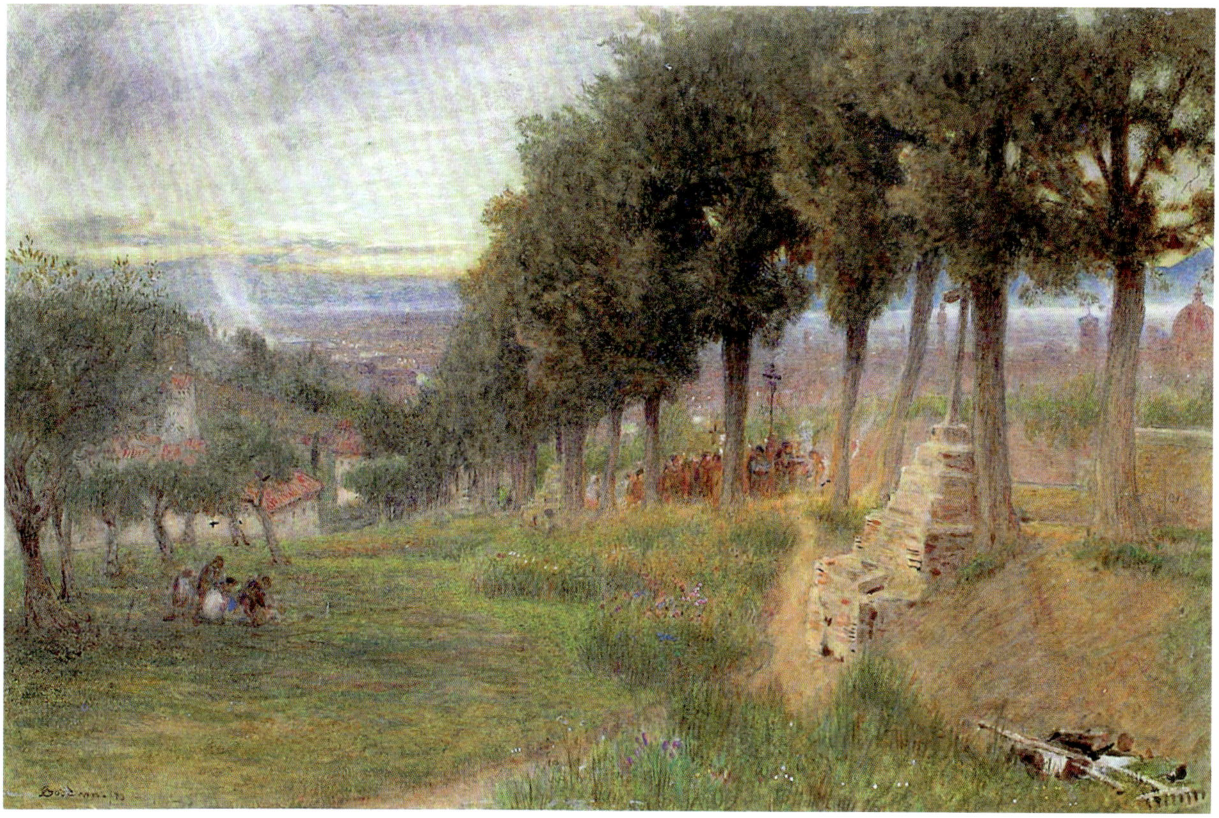

29 VIA CRUCIS, FLORENCE
signed and dated 73
watercolour with bodycolour
8 ¾ x 13 ¾ INCHES

30 DORDRECHT
signed and inscribed with title
watercolour and bodycolour, with decorative border
8 x 11 ½ INCHES

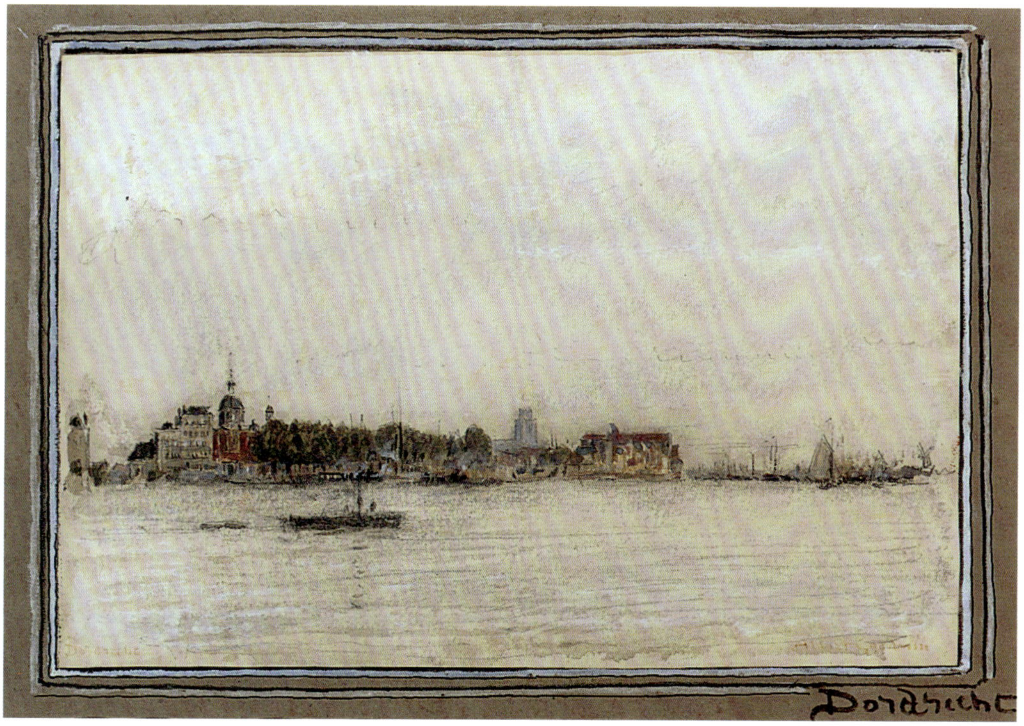

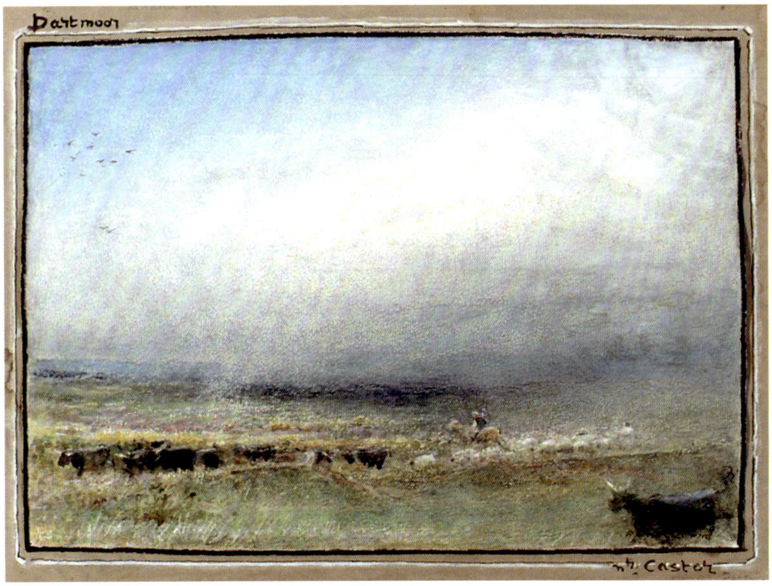

31 DARTMOOR

signed and inscribed with title
watercolour with bodycolour
with decorative border
10 x 14 INCHES

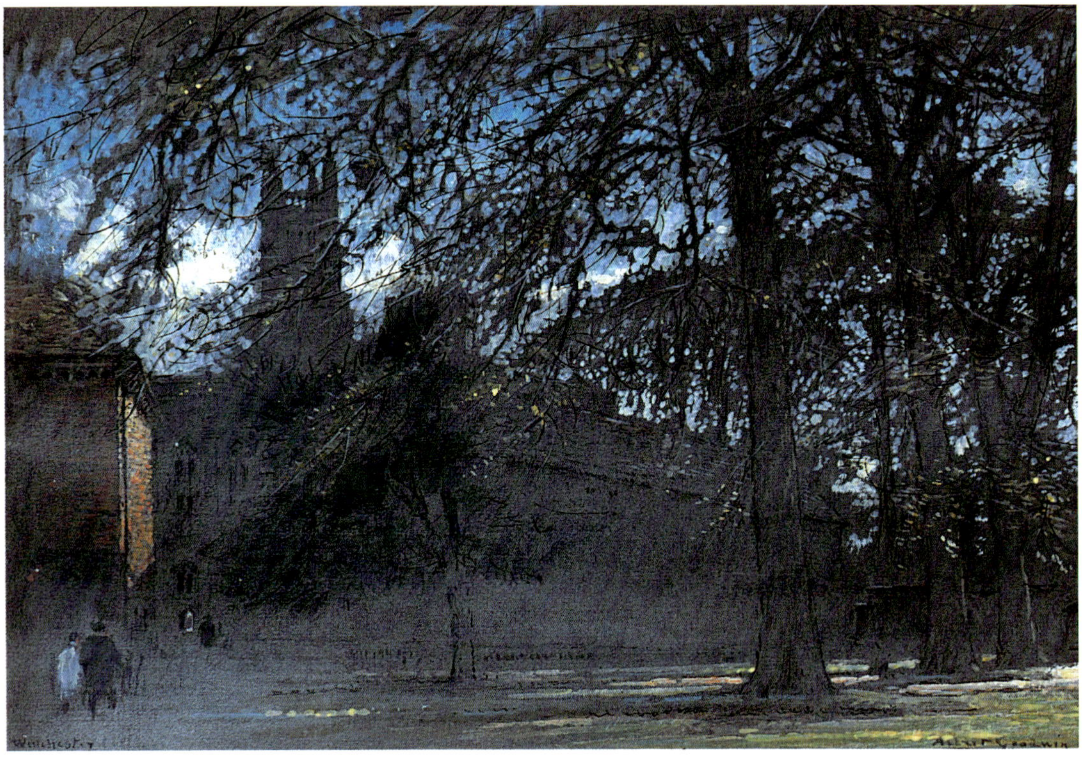

32 WINCHESTER COLLEGE

signed and inscribed with title
pen and ink, watercolour and
bodycolour on tinted paper
10 ¼ x 15 INCHES

LITERATURE: *Albert Goodwin RWS 1845-1932*,
London: Chris Beetles, 1986,
plate 117, limited edition of 1000

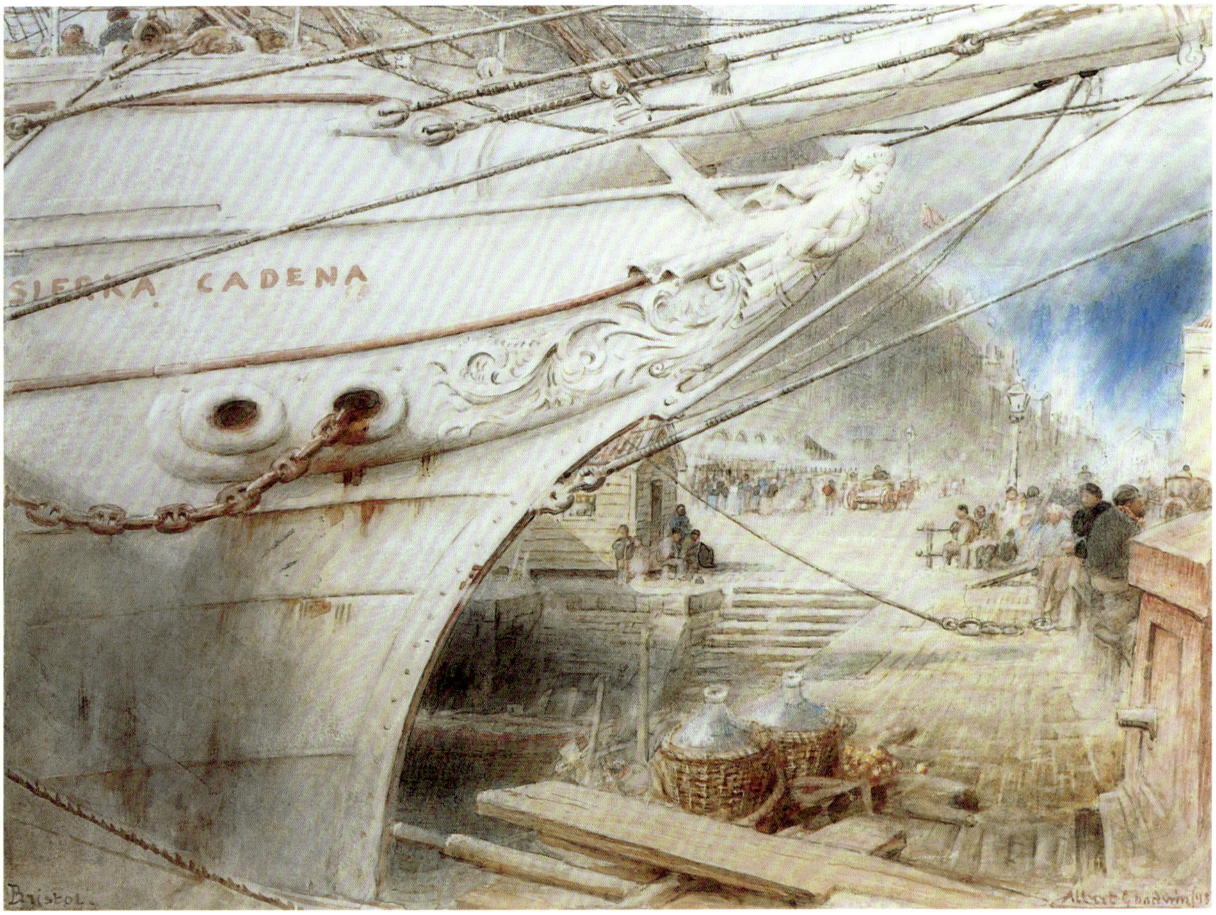

33 BRISTOL
signed, inscribed with title and dated /93
watercolour
9 ¾ x 13 ¼ INCHES

not illustrated
34 THE WALLS OF LUCERNE
signed with monogram and dated '87
pen and ink and watercolour
4 ½ x 6 INCHES

not illustrated
35 DOVER
signed and inscribed with title
watercolour and bodycolour
on tinted paper
7 x 10 INCHES

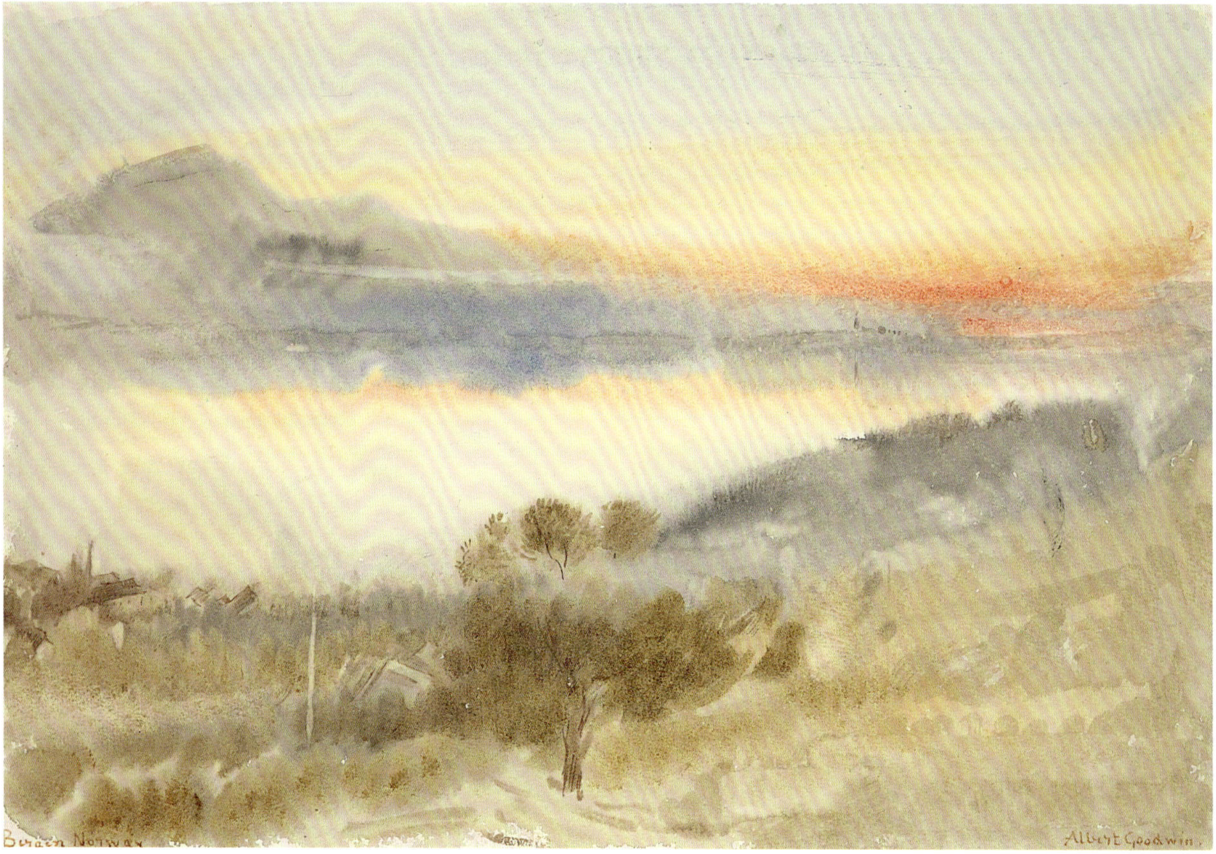

36 BERGEN, NORWAY

signed and inscribed with title

watercolour

10 x 14 INCHES

37 TAJ MAHAL. AGRA

signed and inscribed with title

pen and ink with bodycolour on tinted paper

9 ¾ x 13 ¾ INCHES

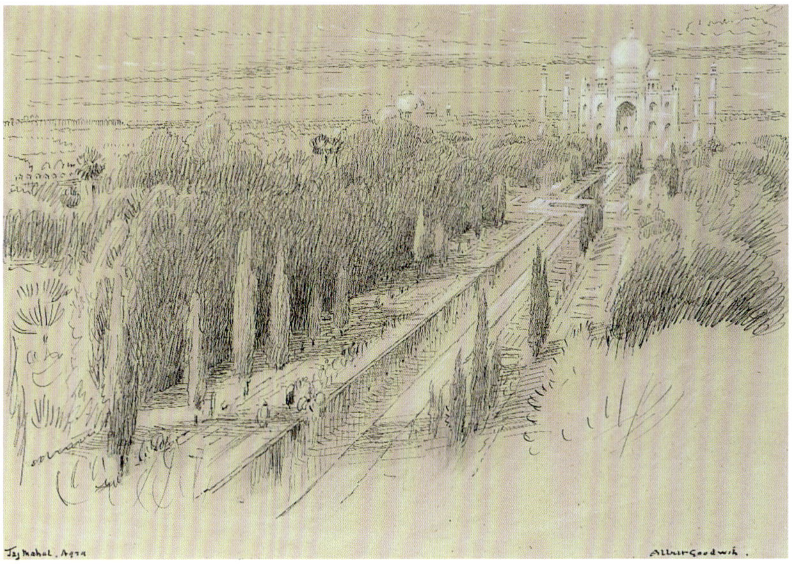

38 OXFORD FROM TRINITY GARDENS

signed and inscribed 'Oxford'

watercolour with pen and ink

10 x 14 INCHES

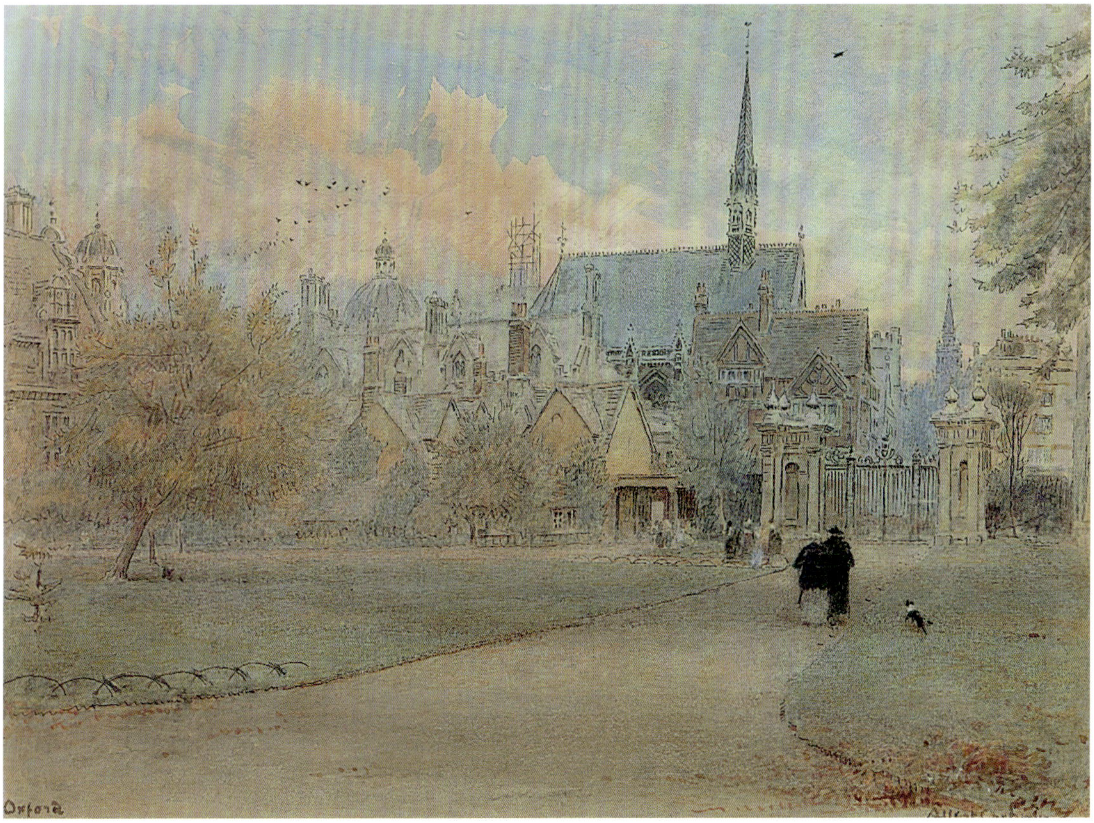

39

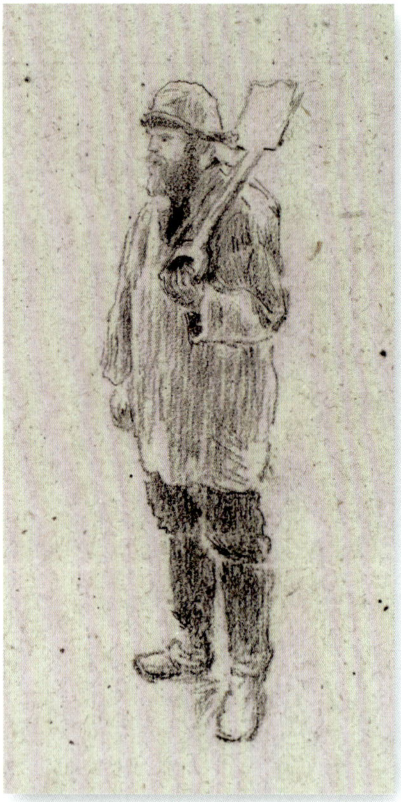

40

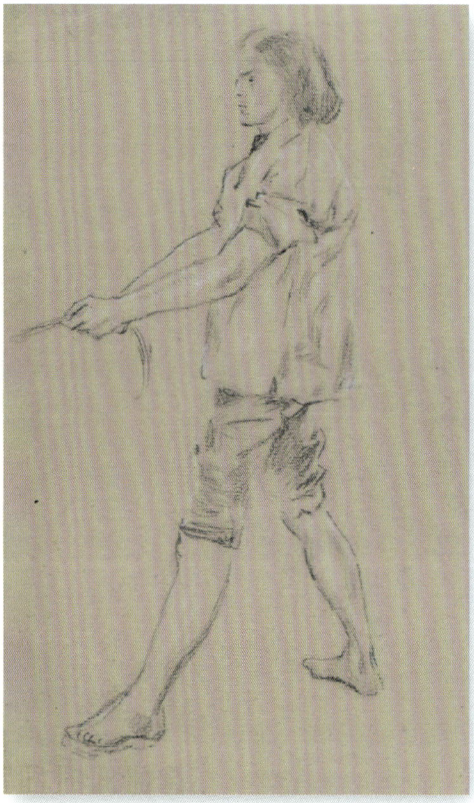

41

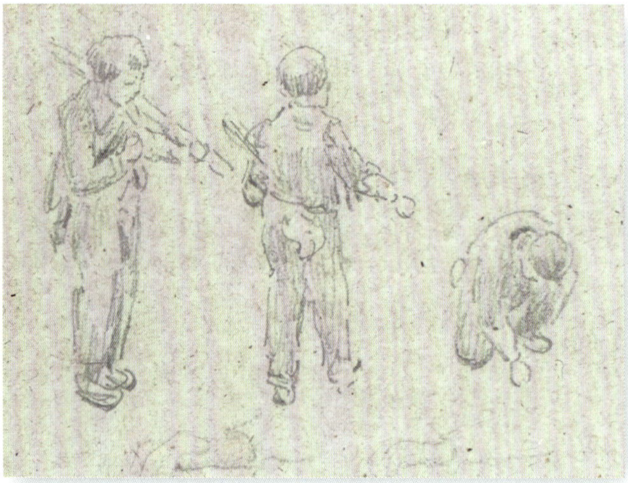

39 LABOURER WITH A SPADE
pencil on tinted paper
10 x 4 INCHES

40 MAN PULLING A ROPE
pencil with white crayon on tinted paper
8 ½ x 5 INCHES

41 STUDY OF THREE CHILDREN
pencil on tinted paper
10 x 12 ½ INCHES

42

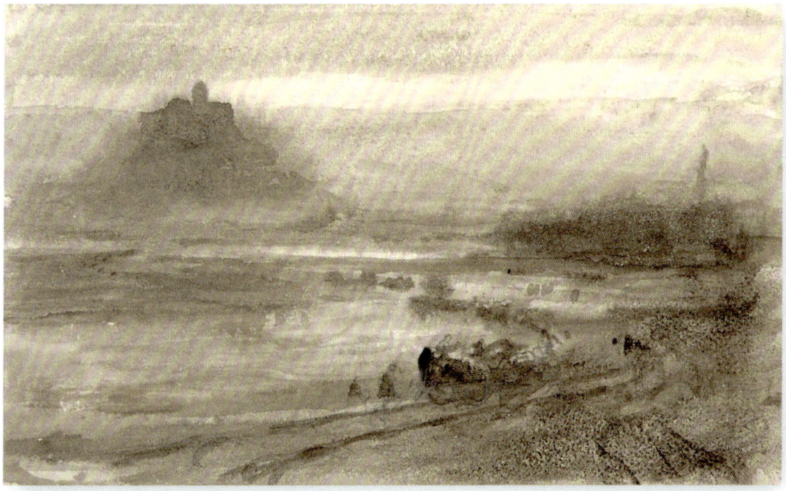

43

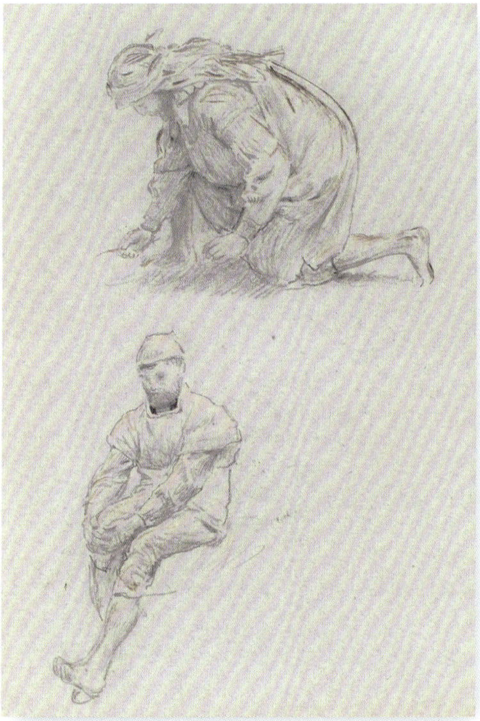

44

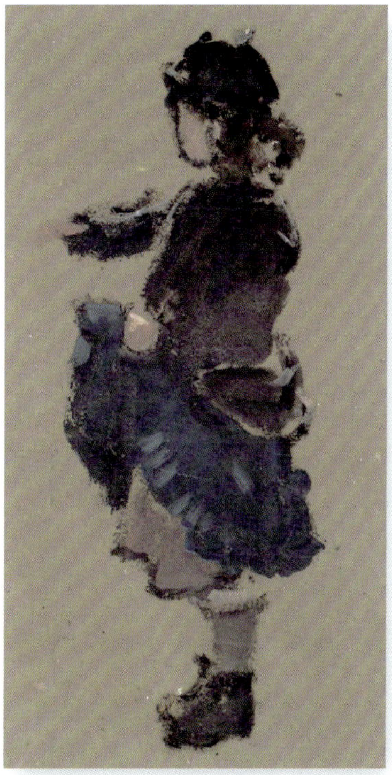

42 ST MICHAELS MOUNT
inscribed with title
monochrome watercolour with pencil
3 ¼ x 6 ½ INCHES
part of a monochrome watercolour drawing inscribed 'first note for "Syren Sea"' on reverse

43 KNEELING AND SEATED FIGURE
pencil with coloured crayon on tinted paper
15 ½ x 10 ½ INCHES

44 SMALL GIRL IN A PETTICOAT
oil on tinted paper
9 x 4 INCHES

45

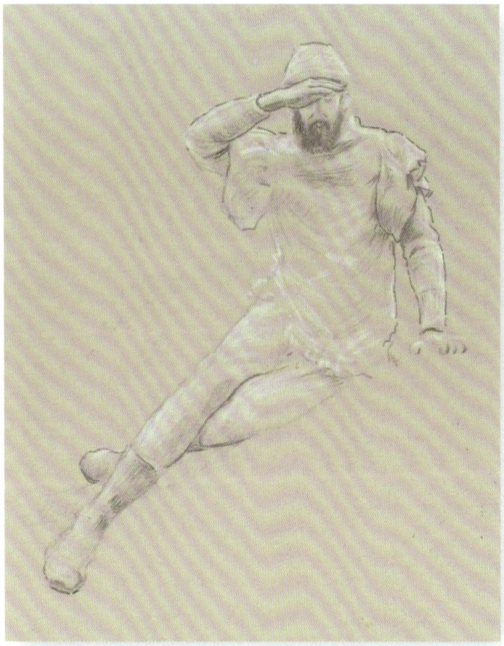

46

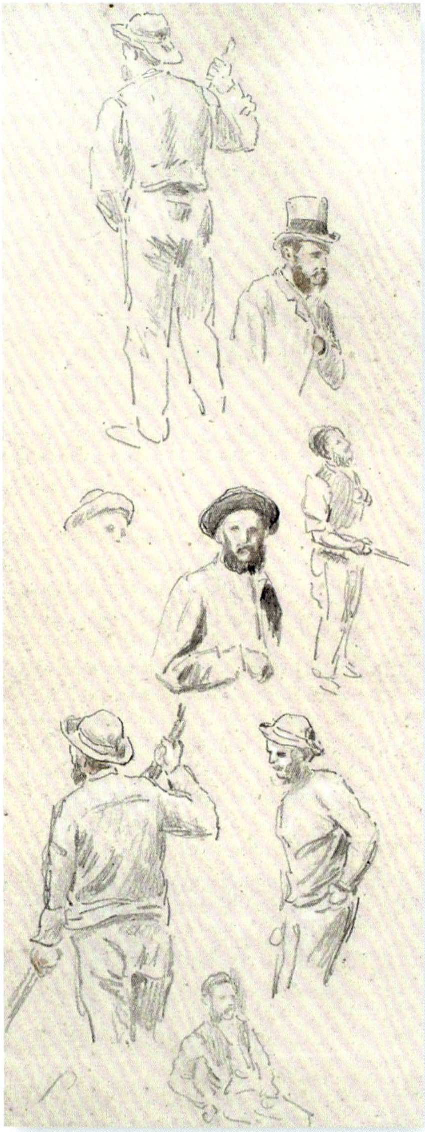

47

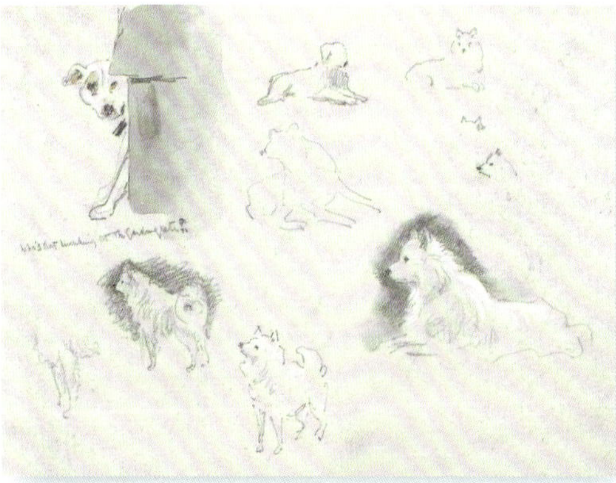

45 LOOKING OUT
pencil and white crayon on tinted paper
10 x 8 ½ INCHES

46 LABOURERS AND A GENTLEMAN IN A TOP HAT
pencil and coloured crayon on tinted paper
13 ¼ x 5 INCHES

47 WHO'S THAT KNOCKING AT THE GARDEN GATE?
signed with initials and inscribed with title
pencil with white crayon on tinted paper
5 x 6 ¾ INCHES

48

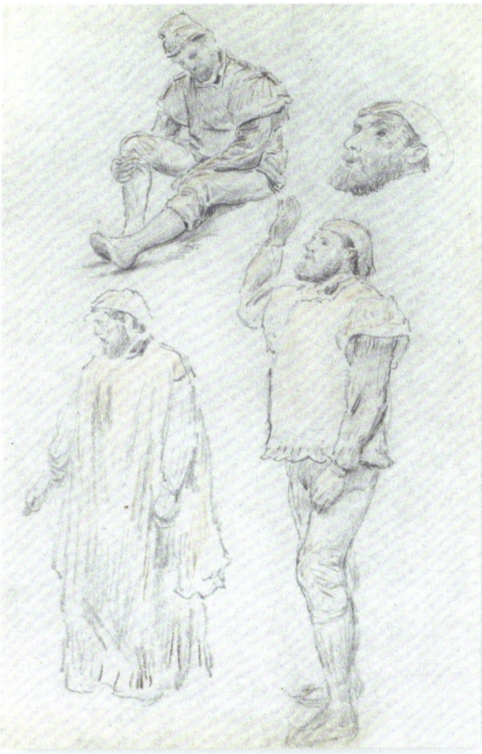

49

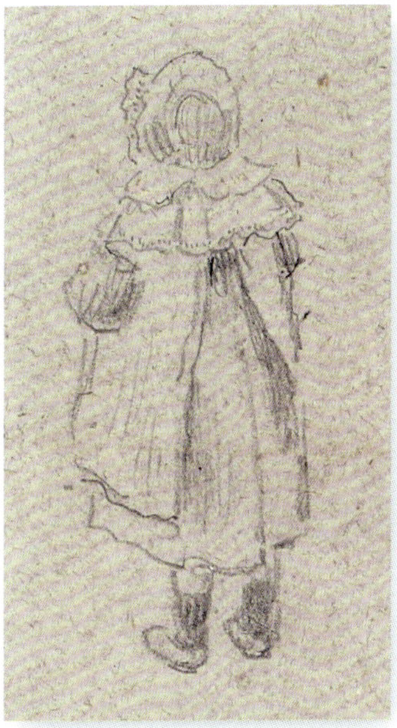

50

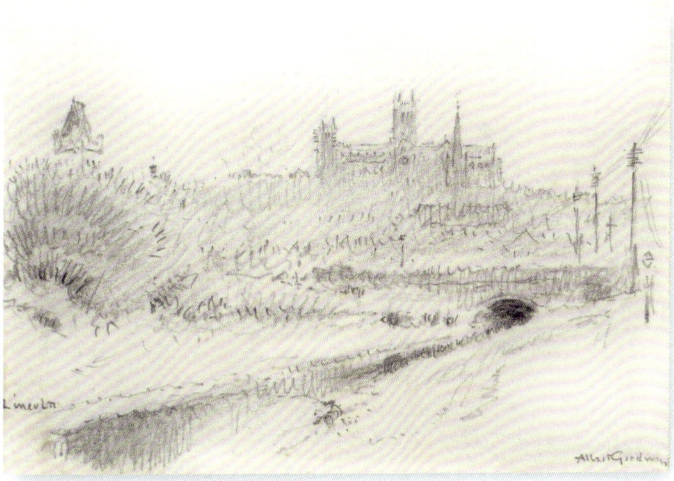

48 THOUGHTFUL FIGURES
pencil and coloured crayon on tinted paper
17 x 11 INCHES

49 STUDIES OF LITTLE GIRLS (detail)
pencil on tinted paper
11 x 7 INCHES

50 LINCOLN
signed and inscribed with title
pencil
5 x $6\frac{3}{4}$ INCHES

51

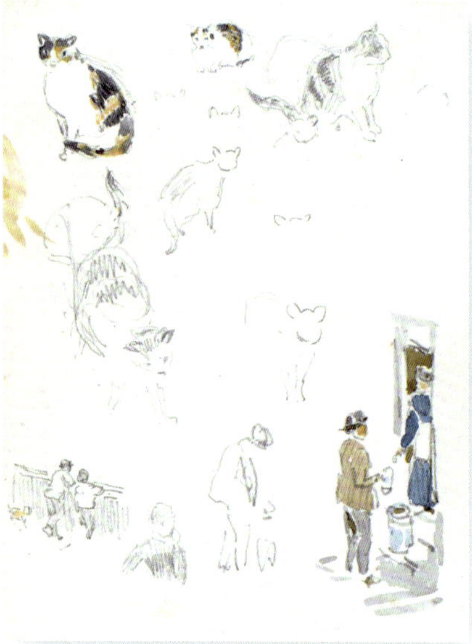

52

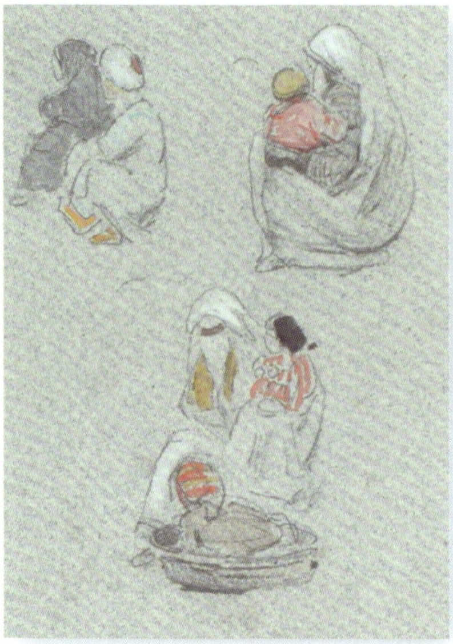

53

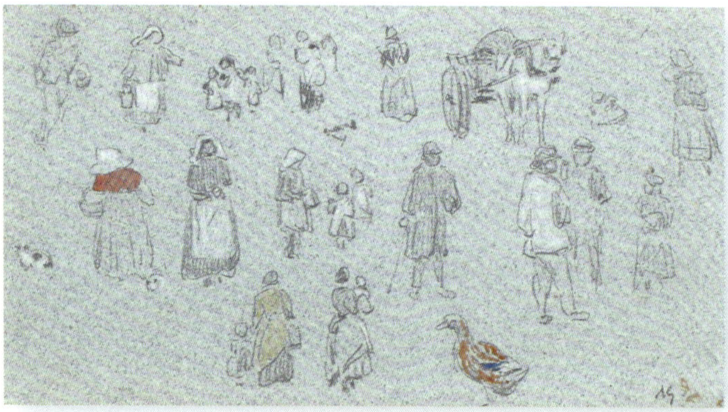

54

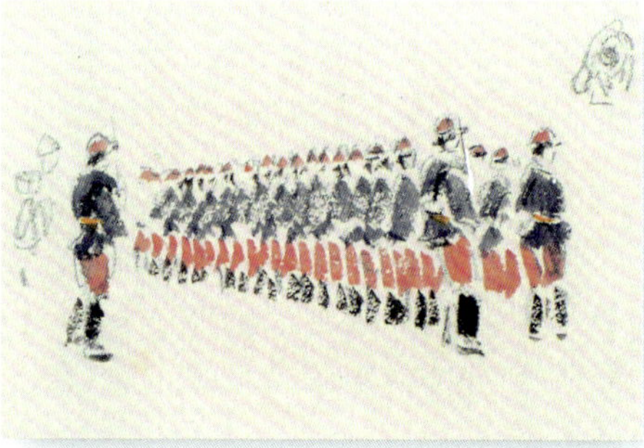

51 CATS AND THE MILKMAN
signed with initials
pencil and watercolour with bodycolour
6 ½ x 5 INCHES

52 CAIRO
signed with initials and inscribed with title
pencil and watercolour on tinted paper
6 ½ x 4 INCHES
drawings of figures in pencil and watercolour on reverse

53 MARKET DAY FIGURES
signed with initials
pencil with watercolour and crayon on tinted paper
4 ½ x 8 ½ INCHES
drawing of a rocky landscape in pencil on reverse

54 SOLDIERS ON PARADE
signed with initials
watercolour and pencil on tinted paper
3 ½ x 4 INCHES

55

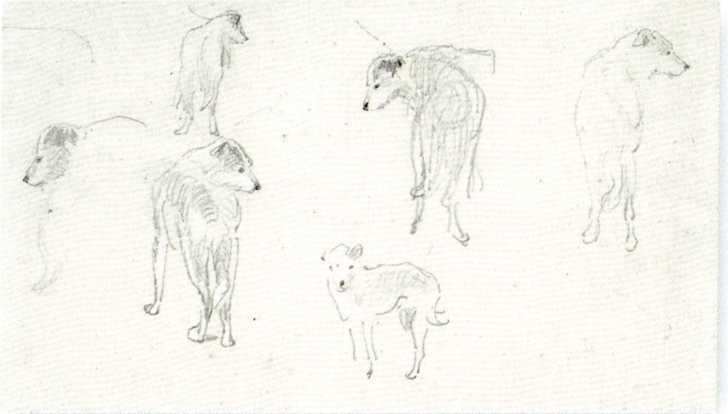

56

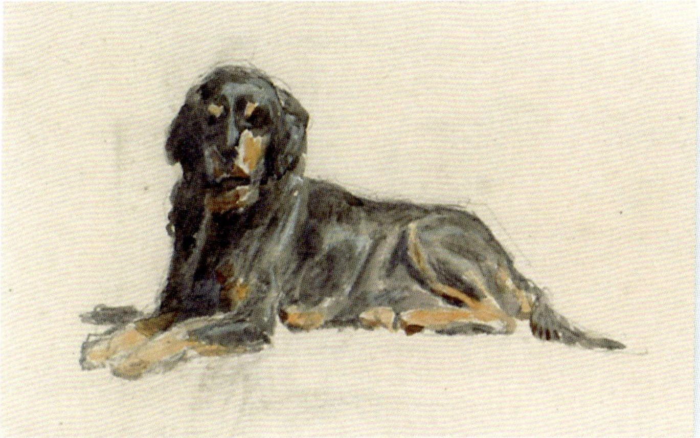

57

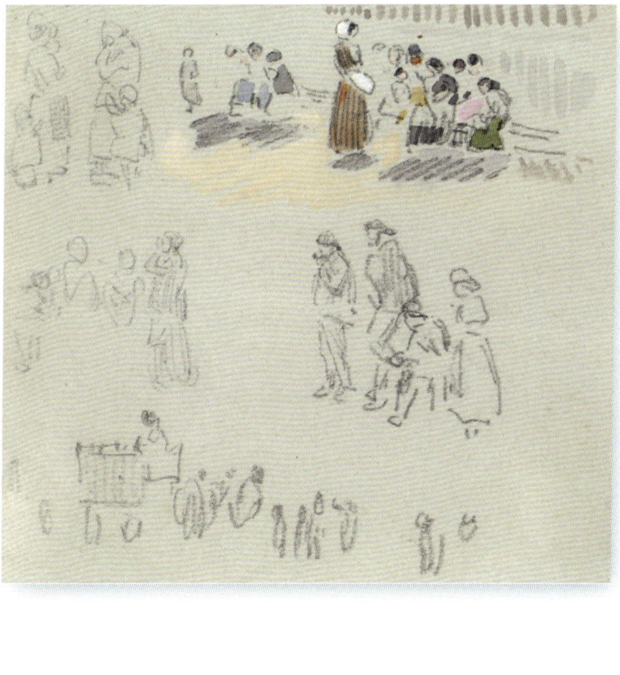

55 SKETCHES OF A LURCHER
pencil with white crayon
4 ½ x 7 ½ INCHES

56 ALERT DOG
signed with initials
watercolour
2 ½ x 4 INCHES

57 CONVERSATIONAL GROUPS
pencil and watercolour
4 ¼ x 5 INCHES

58

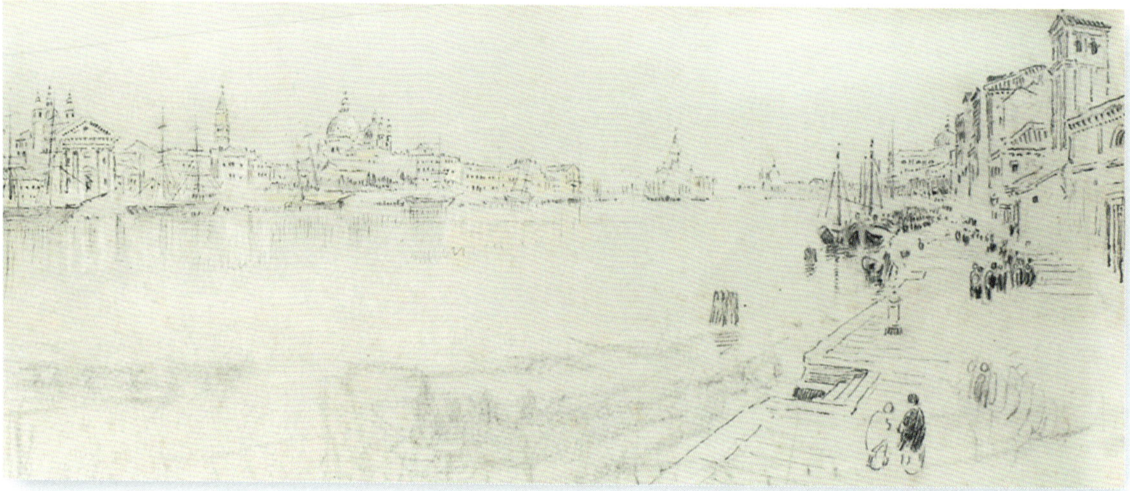

59

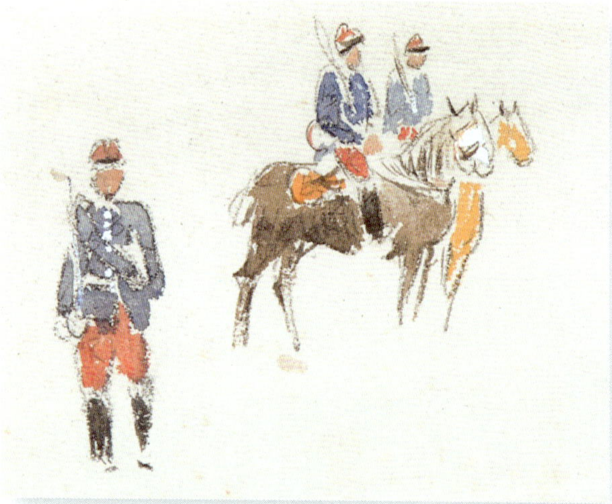

60

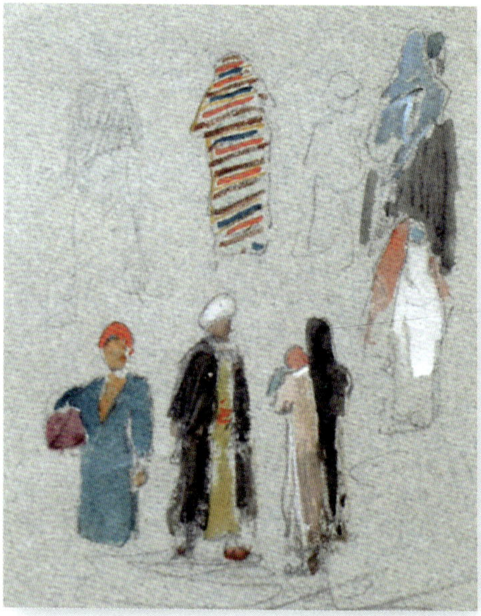

58 VENICE FROM THE GIUDECCA
pen and ink and pencil
4 ¼ x 10 INCHES

59 CAVALRY MEN
signed with initials
watercolour and pencil on tinted paper
2 ½ x 3 INCHES

60 CAIRO (detail)
signed with initials and inscribed with title
watercolour and pencil on tinted paper
6 ½ x 4 INCHES

61 DORKING FAIR

signed with initials, inscribed 'Dorking' and artists notes
pencil, watercolour with bodycolour on tinted paper
5 x 6 ½ INCHES

61

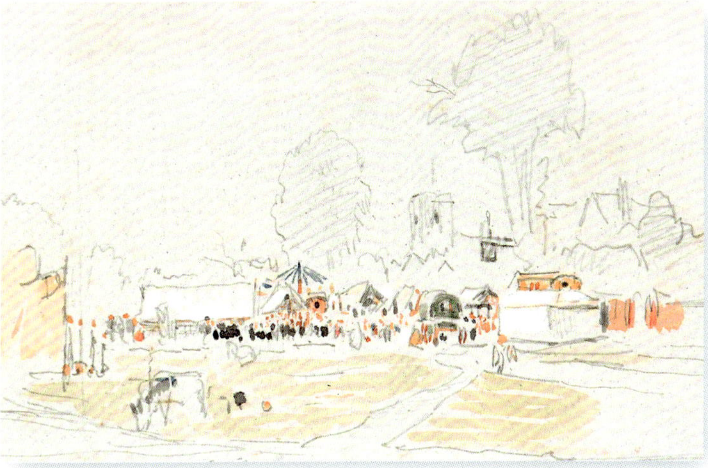

62 VENICE THE TENDERING OF THE STORK FISH

signed with initials and inscribed with title
pencil on tinted paper
5 ½ x 8 ½ INCHES

62

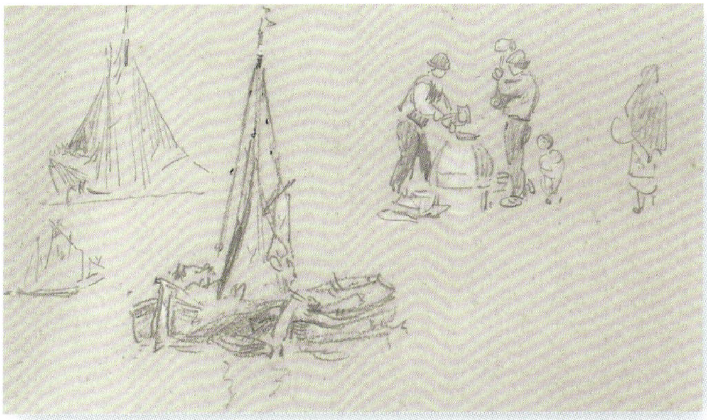

63 ST VINCENT PORTSMOUTH & GUN BOAT

inscribed with title
pencil on tinted paper
5 ¼ x 6 ½ INCHES
drawing of a landscape in pencil on reverse

63

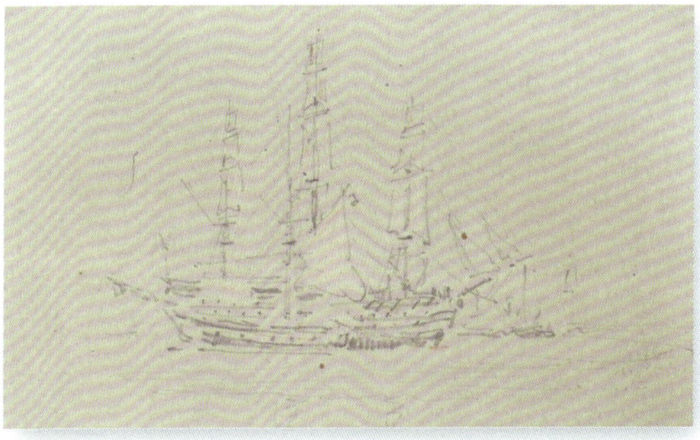

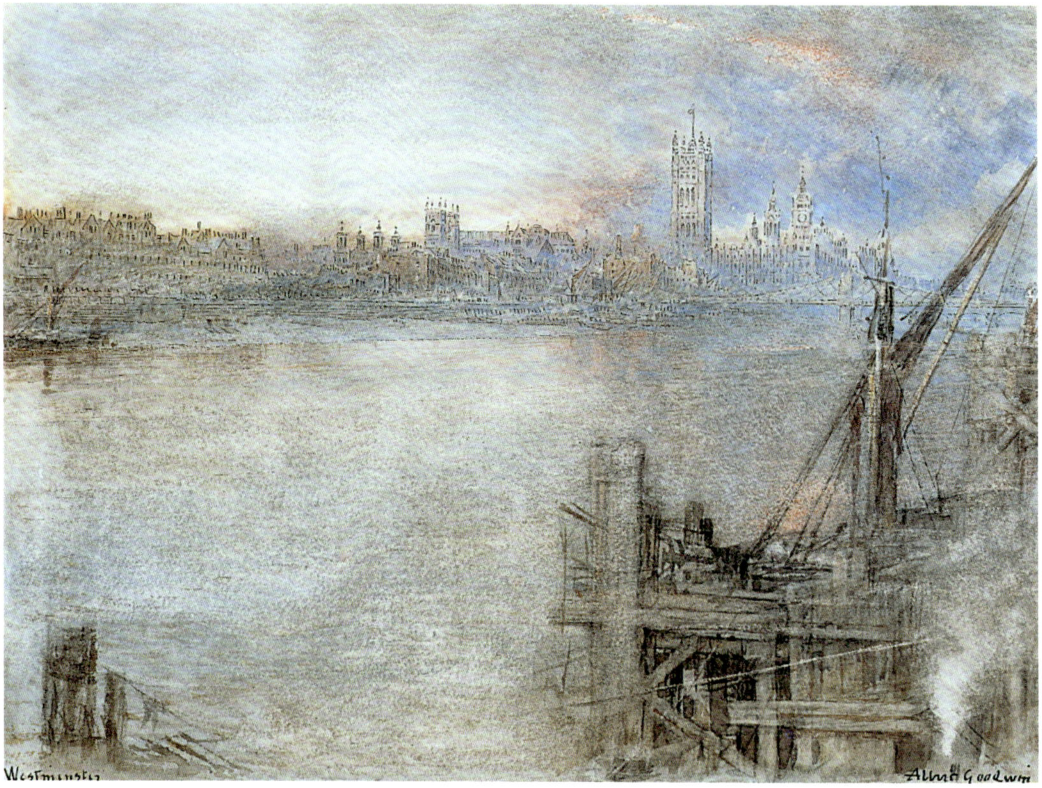

64 WESTMINSTER
signed and inscribed with title
watercolour
9 x 12 INCHES

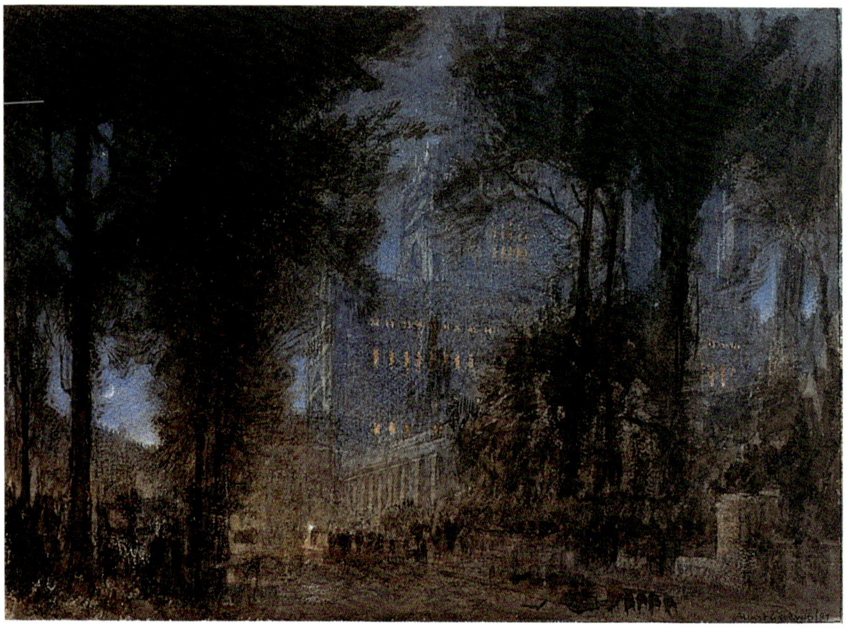

65 THE EVENING SERVICE, SALISBURY
signed and dated '97
watercolour
9 x 12 ½ INCHES

66 BENARES (opposite)
signed, inscribed with title and dated 1899
oil on canvas
38 ½ x 24 INCHES

EXHIBITED: Royal Academy of Arts, London, 1899, no 224

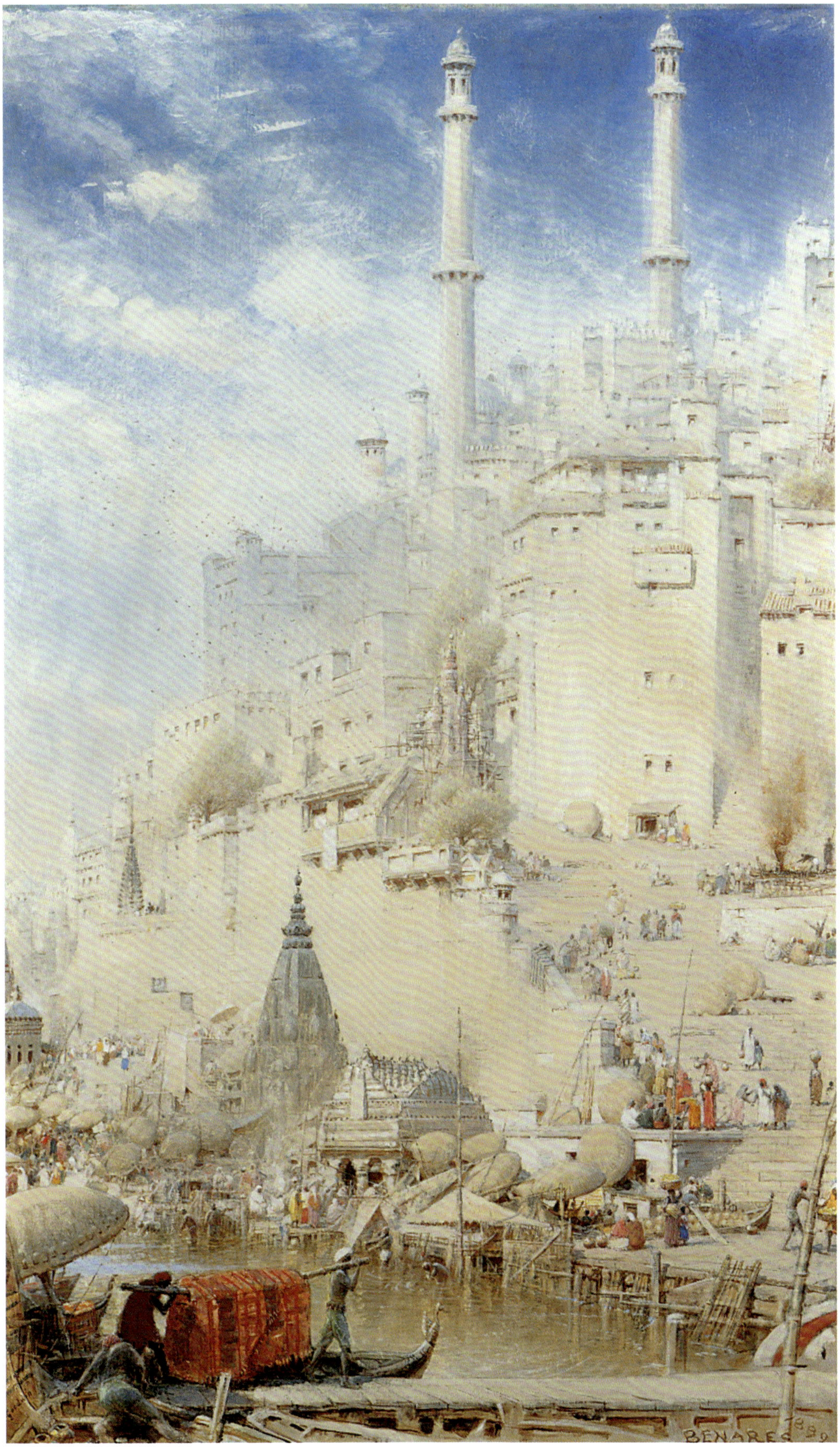
BENARES 1889

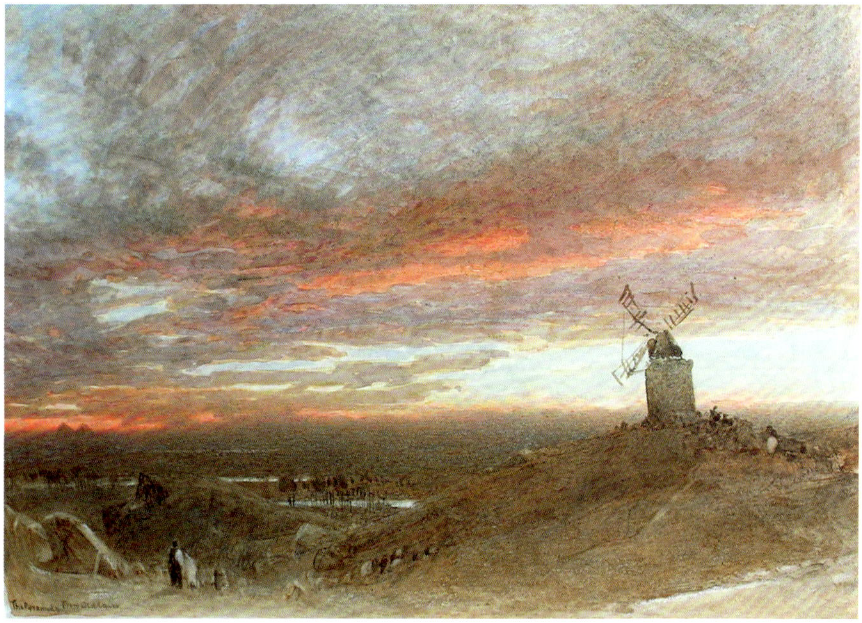

67 THE PYRAMIDS FROM OLD CAIRO

signed, inscribed with title and dated 98
watercolour
10 x 14 ¼ INCHES

EXHIBITED: 'A Collection of Pictures and Sketches including a series of Whitby and "The First Christmas Dawn" by Albert Goodwin, RWS', Fine Art Society, London, 1898, no 59 as 'The Last of the Windmills, Cairo'

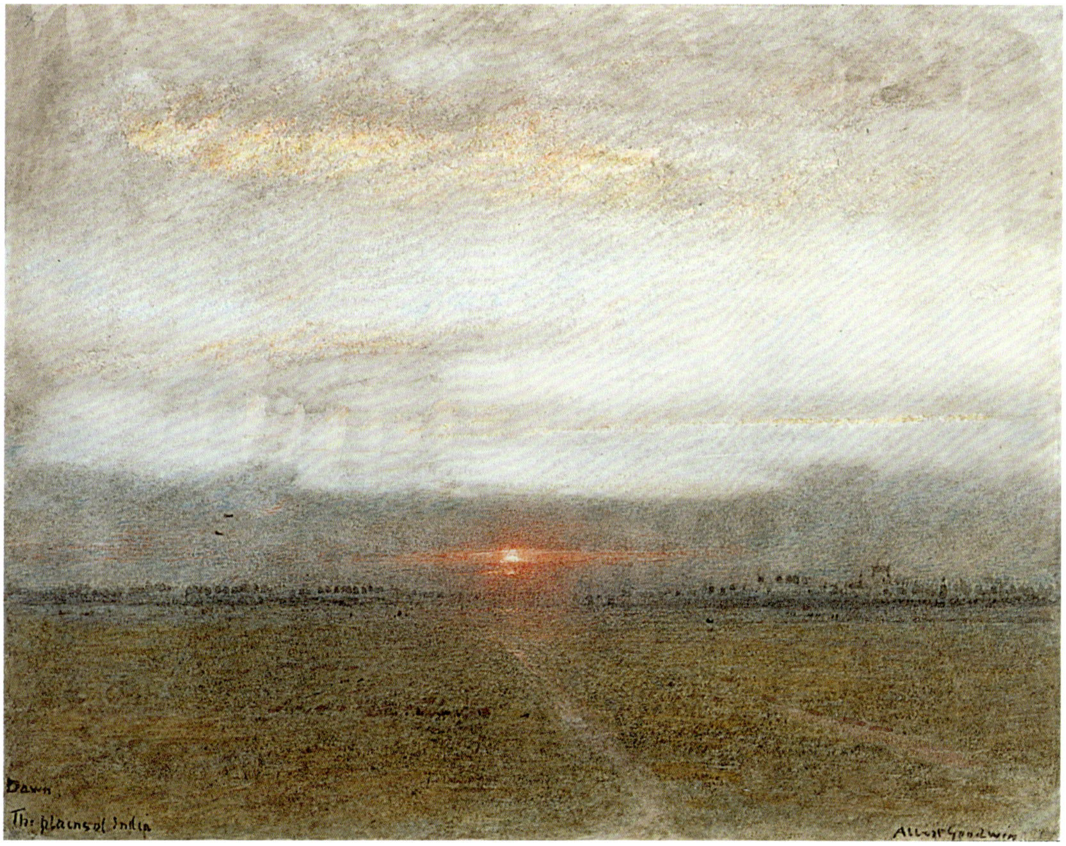

68 DAWN. THE PLAINS OF INDIA

signed and inscribed with title
watercolour
9 ½ x 12 INCHES

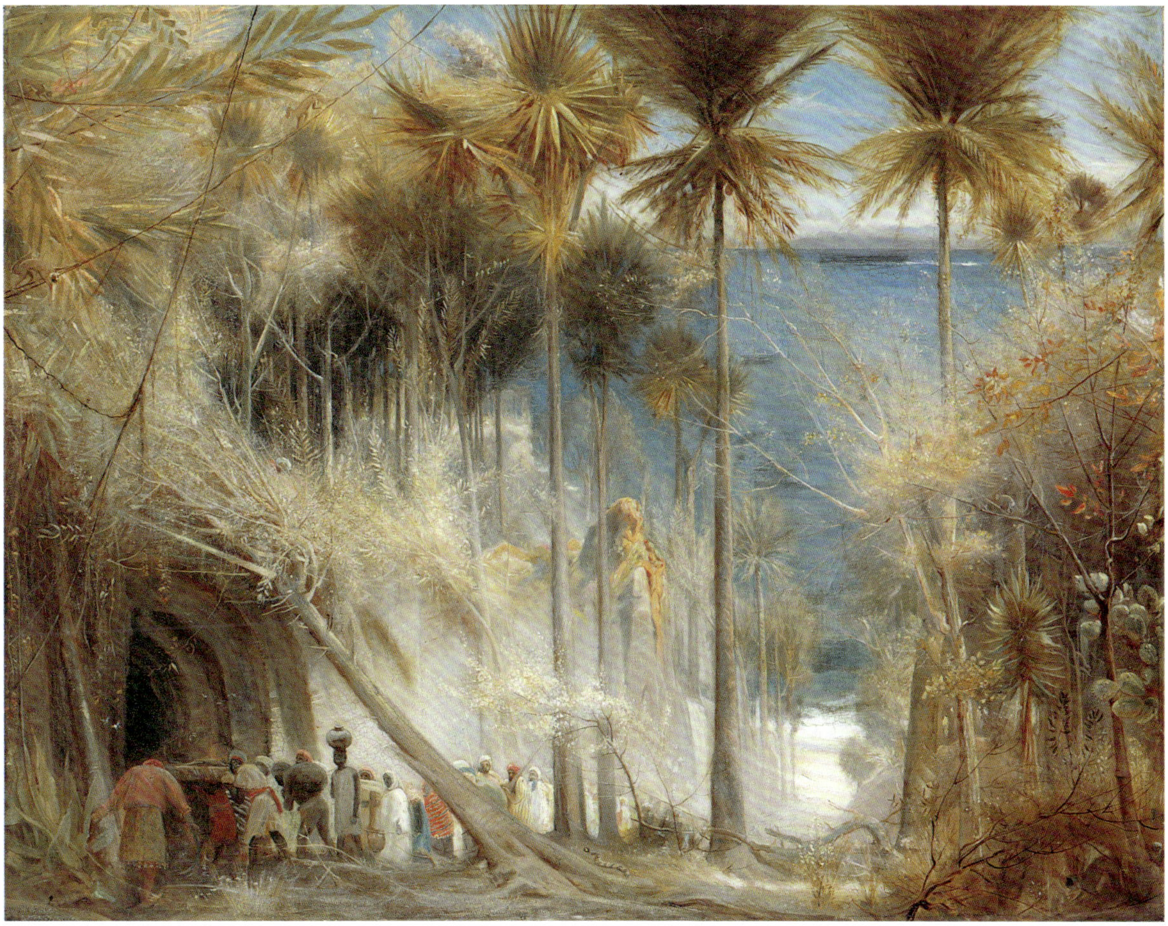

69 ALI BABA AND THE FORTY THIEVES

inscribed with title
oil on canvas
30 ¾ x 40 INCHES

An identical, though larger version of this painting (41 ¾ x 55 inches) was exhibited at the Royal Academy Summer Exhibition in 1901 (no 53, purchased by the Chantry Bequest for 300 gns and now in the collection of Tate Britain). The present painting was most likely a commission, executed at a slightly reduced scale to meet the requirements of the patron.

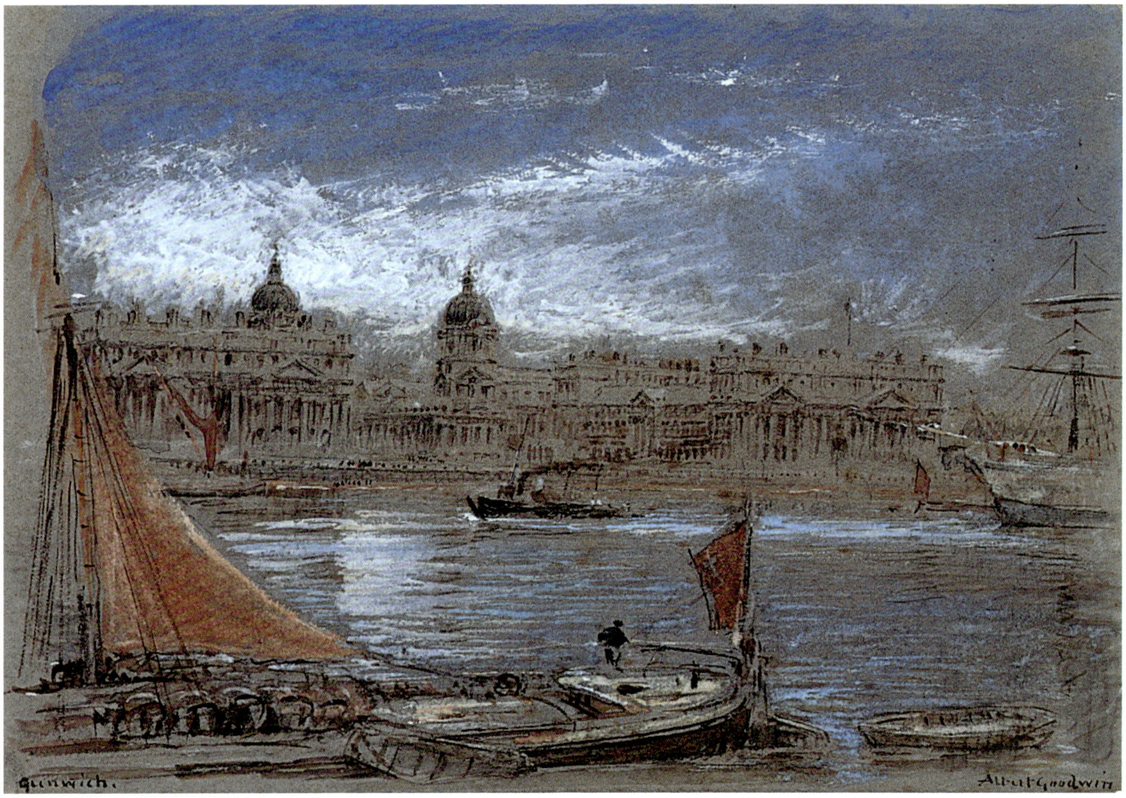

70 GREENWICH

signed and inscribed with title
watercolour and bodycolour
on tinted paper
8 ¼ x 12 ¼ inches

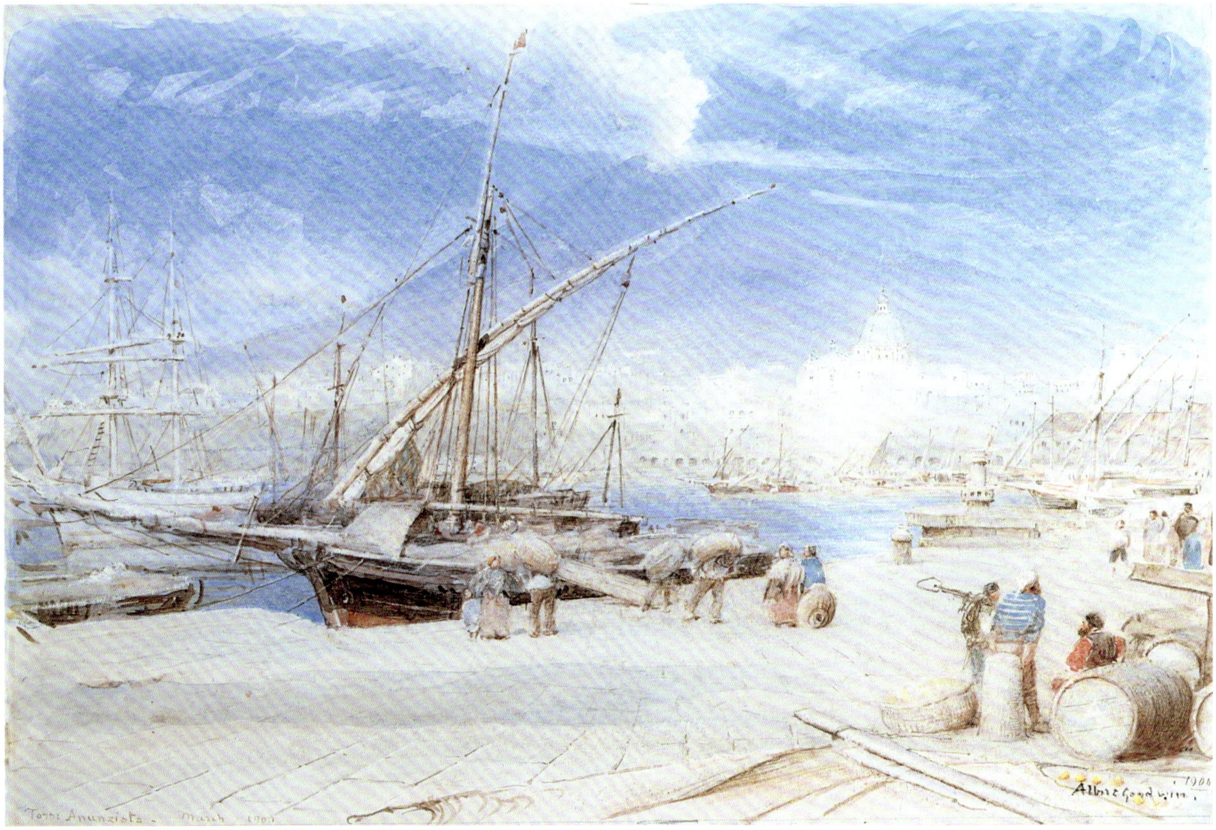

71 TORRE ANUNZIATA

signed, inscribed with title and dated 'March 1900'

watercolour with pen and ink

10 x 14 ¼ INCHES

EXHIBITED: Fine Art Society, November 1900, no 9, as 'Torre Anunziata, Near Naples'

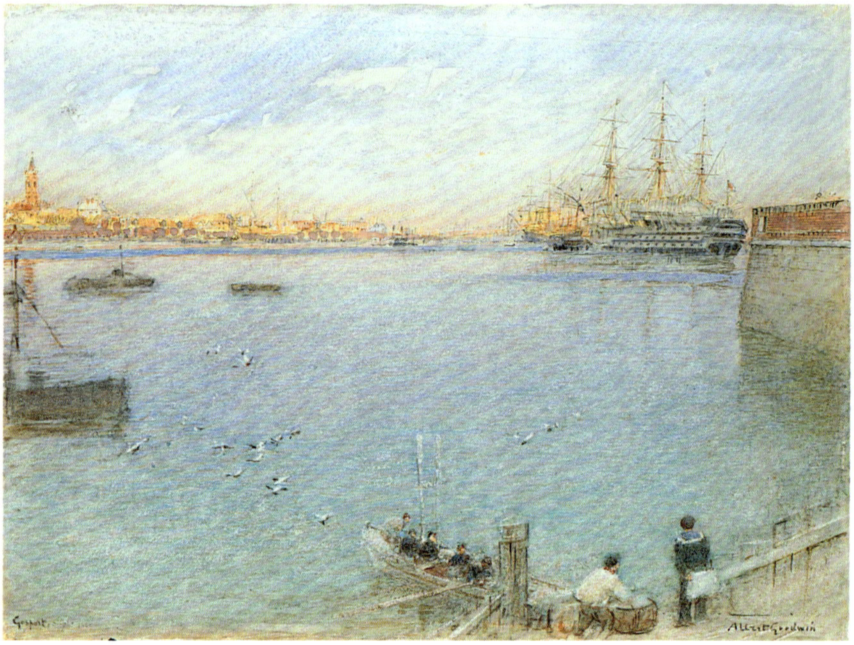

72 HMS VICTORY AT GOSPORT

signed, inscribed 'Gosport' and dated 'Sept 1901'
watercolour with pen and ink and bodycolour
9 x 12 ¼ INCHES

73 BOSTON, LINCOLNSHIRE

signed and inscribed with title
pen and ink and watercolour
7 x 10 ½ INCHES

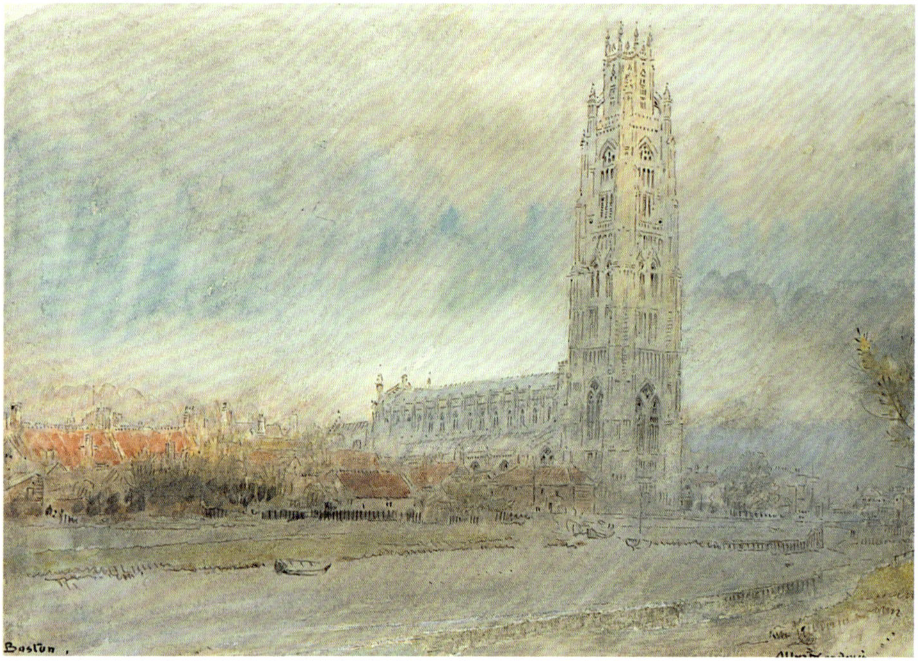

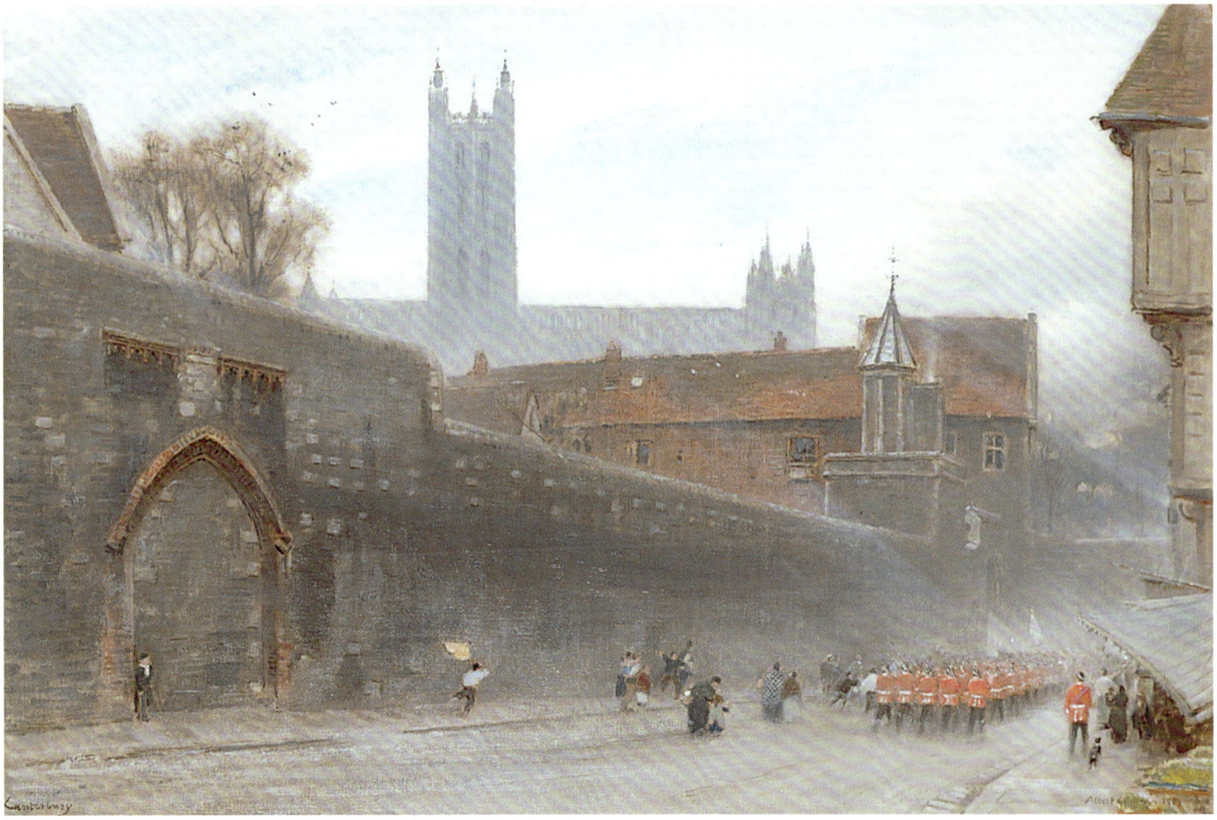

74 CANTERBURY
signed, inscribed with title and dated 1901
oil on canvas
30 ½ x 47 ½ inches

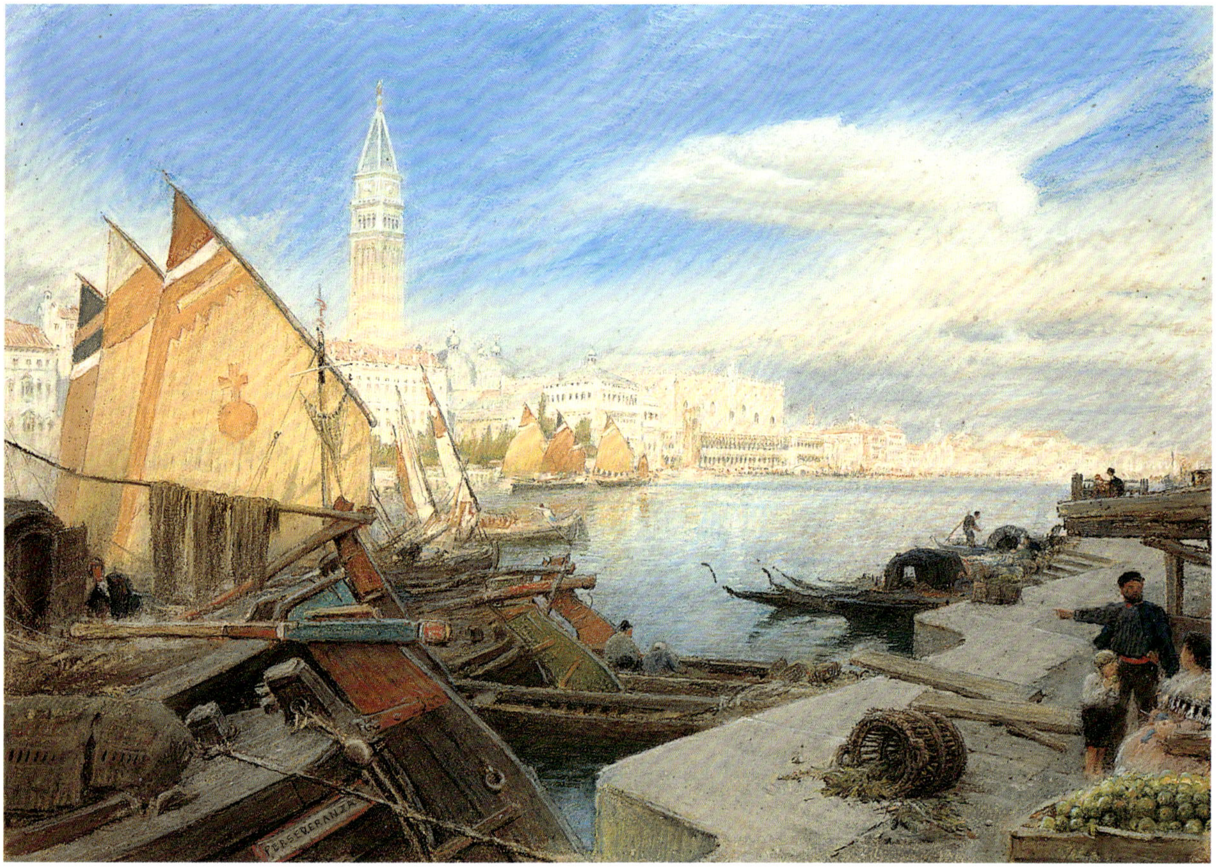

75 VENICE BEFORE THE FALL OF THE CAMPANILE

signed and inscribed 'Venezia'
pastel
21 x 30 ½ INCHES

EXHIBITED: Royal Society Of Painters in Water-Colours, Winter 1902, no 10 as 'Venice Before the Fall of the Tower'

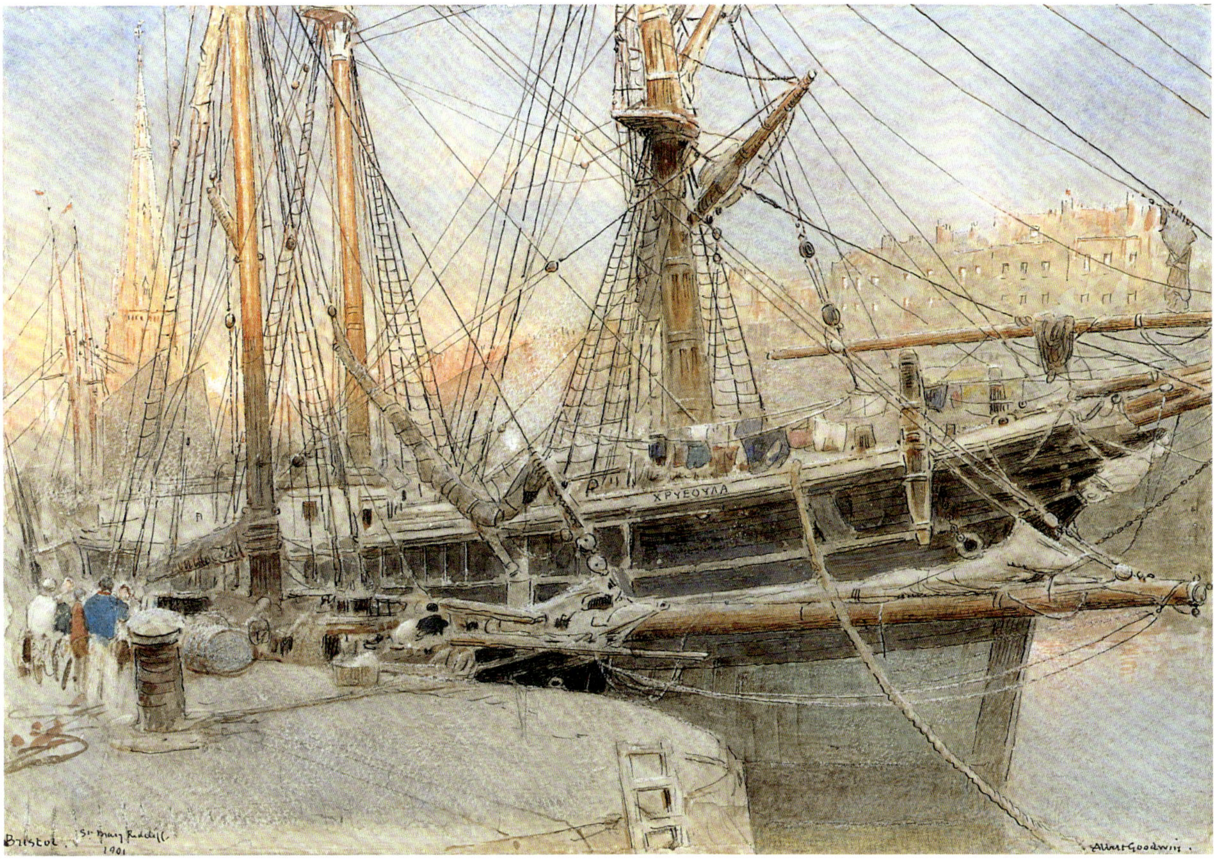

76 BRISTOL.
ST MARY REDCLIFFE

signed, inscribed with title and dated 1901
watercolour with pen and ink
10 x 14 ¾ INCHES

EXHIBITED: 'The Scottish Fine Arts and Print Club Loan Exhibition', Royal Scottish Adademy Galleries, Edinburgh, 1937 (lent by Sir John Stirling Maxwell, BART KT)

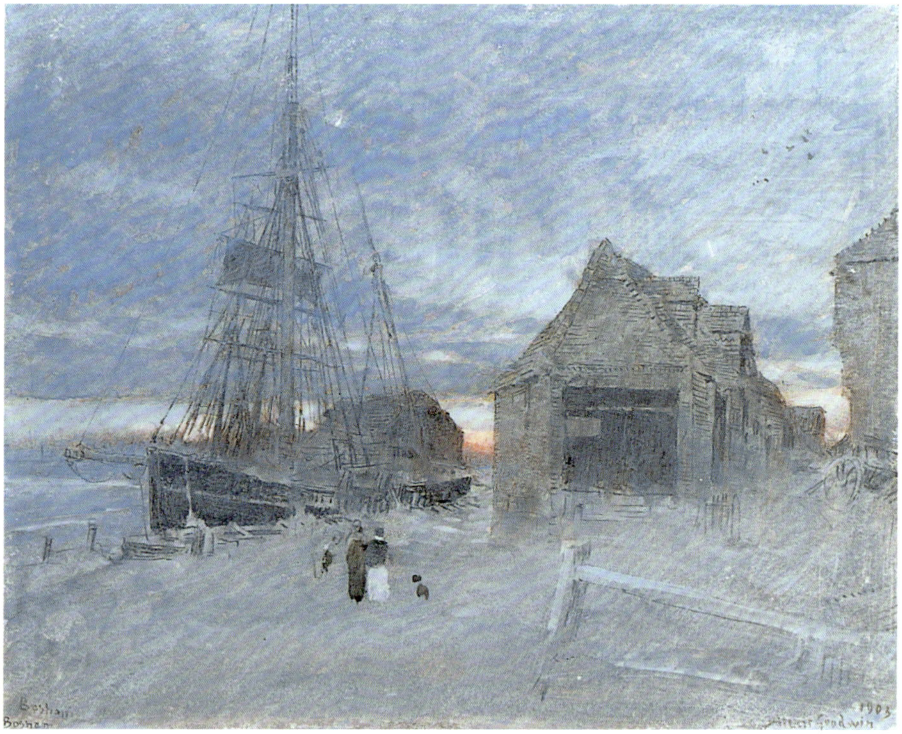

77 BOSHAM

signed, inscribed with title twice and dated 1903
watercolour and bodycolour
9 ¾ x 12 ¼ INCHES

EXHIBITED: 'Water Colour Drawings by Albert Goodwin RWS', Robert Dunthorne's The Rembrant Head Gallery, London, 1904, no 37

78 CANTERBURY. AUTUMN SUNSET

signed, inscribed with title and dated 1903
watercolour with bodycolour and pen and ink on tinted paper
9 ¾ x 14 ¾ INCHES

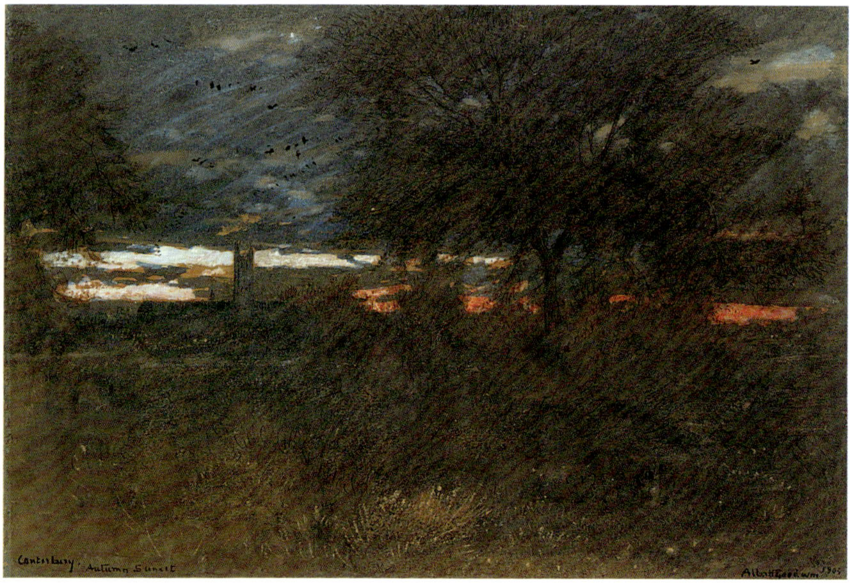

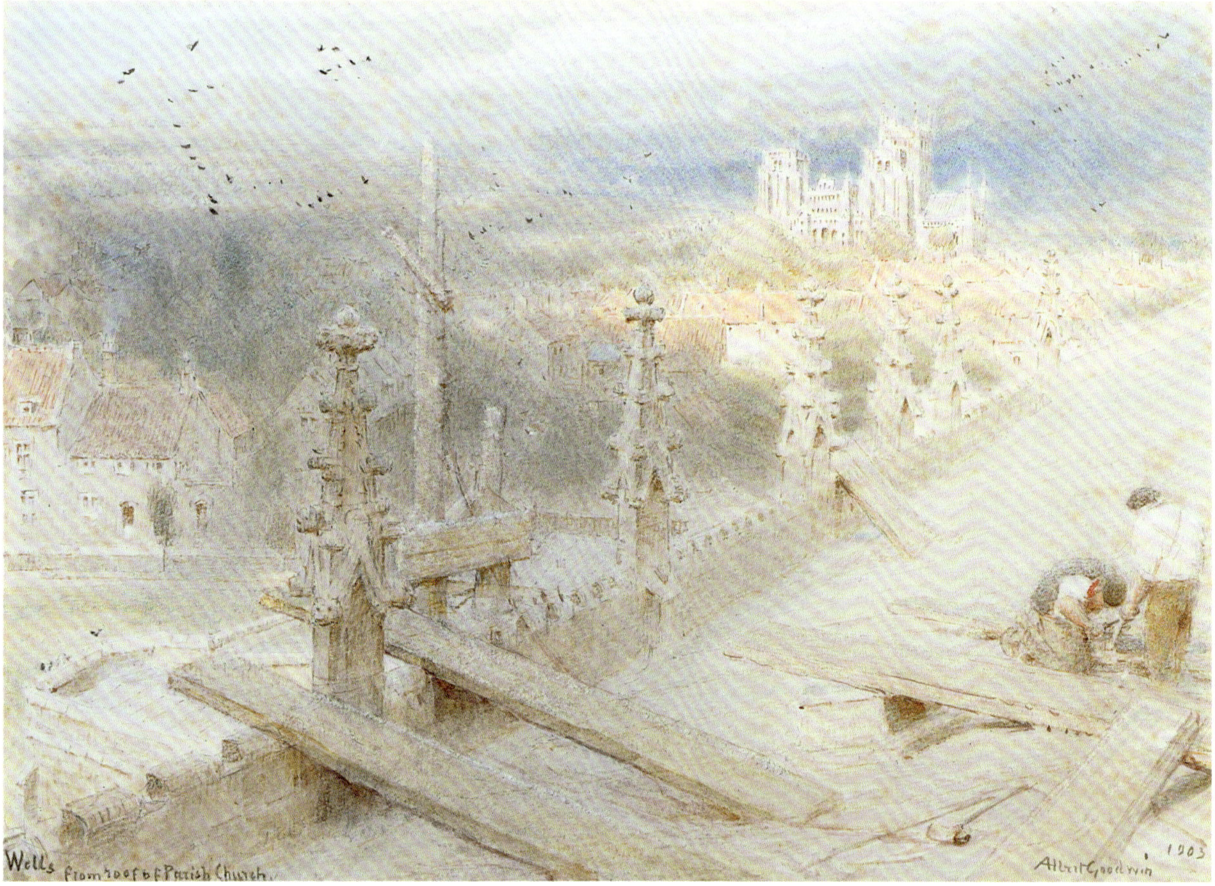

79 WELLS FROM ROOF OF PARISH CHURCH

signed, inscribed with title and dated 1903
watercolour with pencil
10 ¼ x 14 ¼ INCHES

LITERATURE: *Albert Goodwin RWS 1845-1932*, London: Chris Beetles, 1986, plate 79, limited edition of 1000

EXHIBITED: 'Albert Goodwin, RWS 1845-1932', Touring Exhibition, May-October 1986, no 54

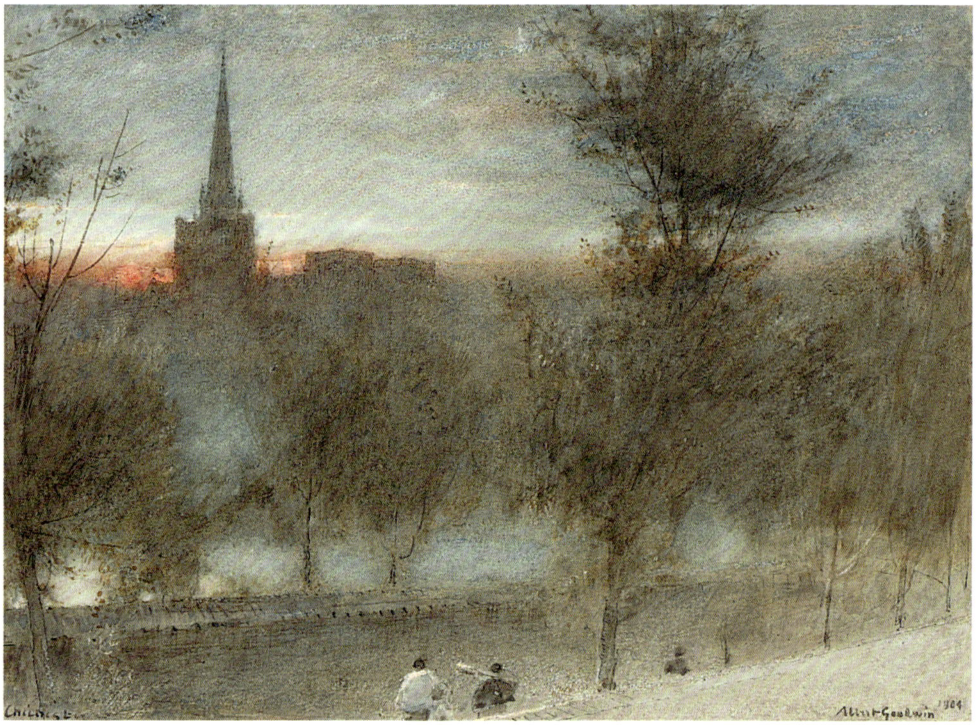

80 CHICHESTER

signed, inscribed with title and dated 1904
watercolour with pen and ink
8 ¼ x 12 INCHES

EXHIBITED: 'Albert Goodwin, RWS 1845-1932', Touring Exhibition, May-October 1986, no 61

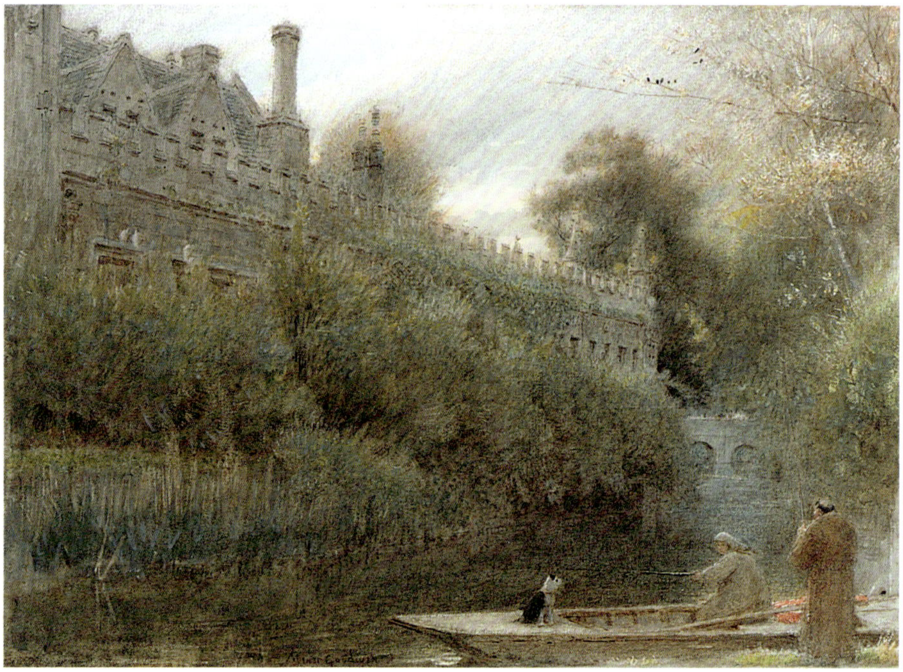

81 ADDISON'S WALK, MAGDALEN COLLEGE, OXFORD

signed
watercolour with pen and ink
10 x 13 ¾ INCHES

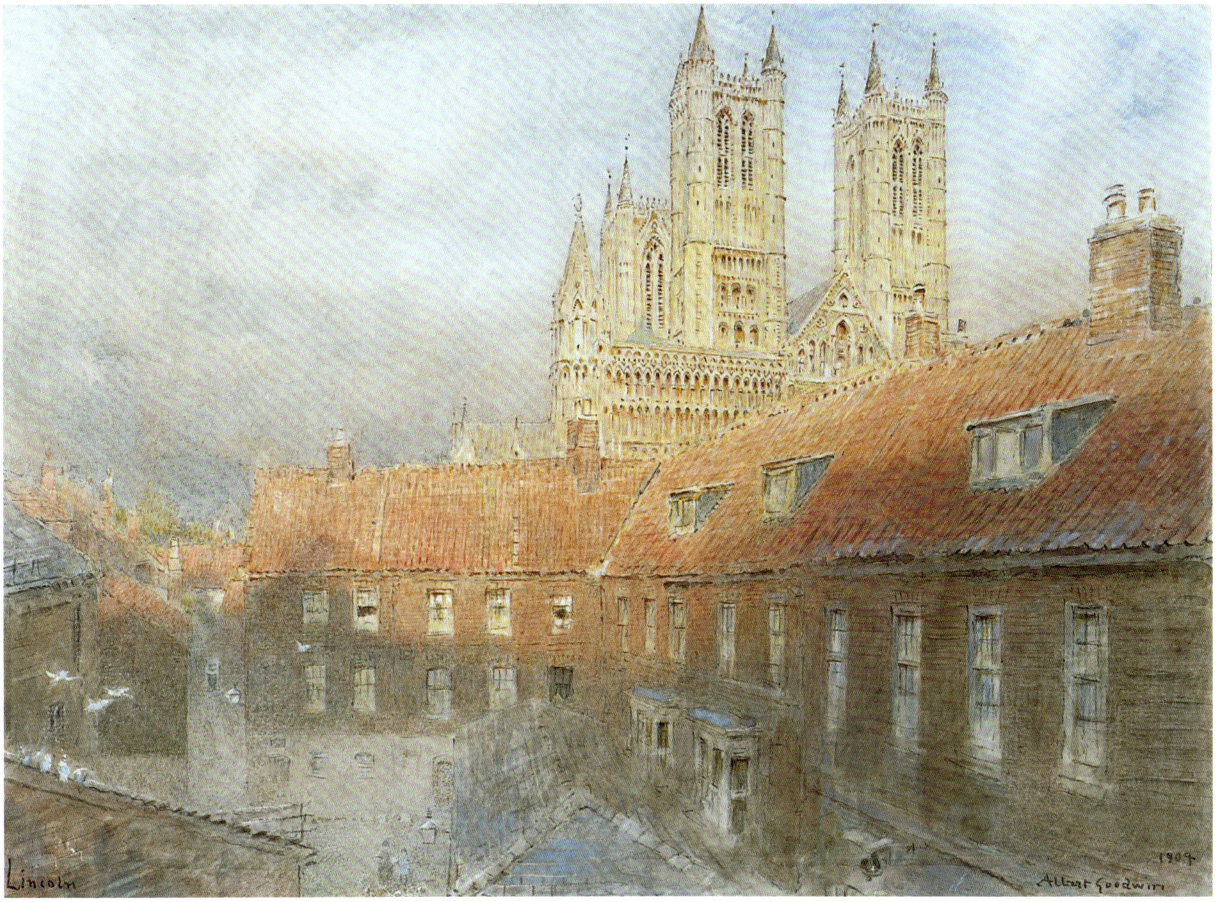

82 LINCOLN

signed, inscribed with title and dated 1904
watercolour with pen and ink
10 ¼ x 14 ¼ INCHES

A painting of this title was exhibited at the Royal Society of Painters in Water-Colours, Winter 1904, no 46

83 VESUVIUS

signed and inscribed with title

pen and ink with bodycolour on tinted paper with decorative border

8 ¼ x 10 ¾ INCHES

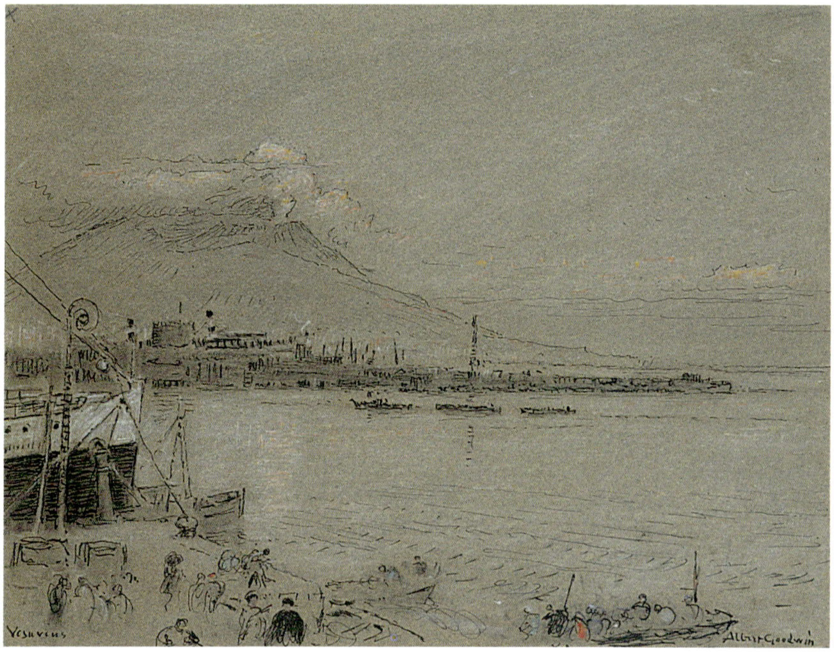

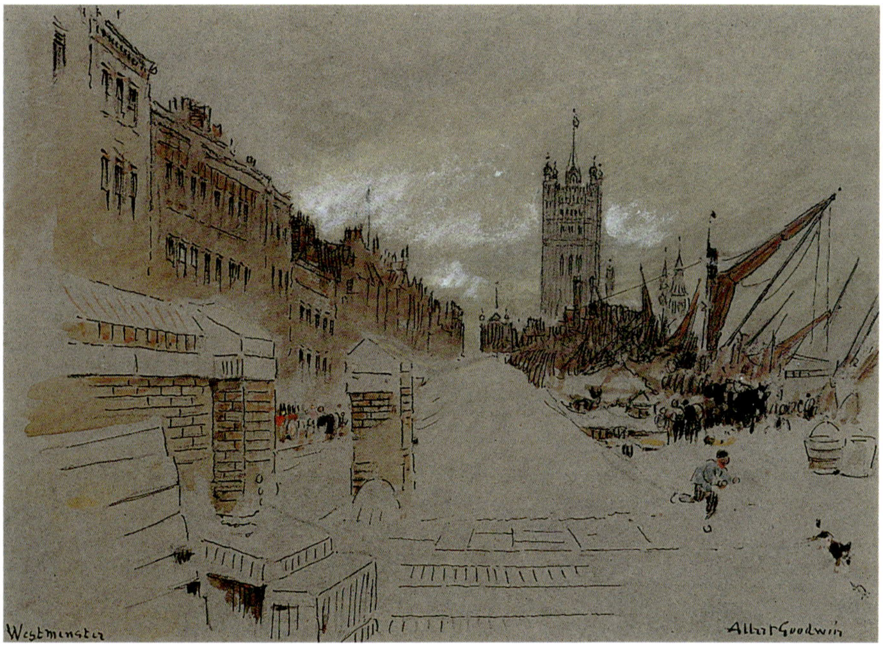

84 WESTMINSTER

signed and inscribed with title

watercolour, pen and ink and bodycolour on tinted paper

7 ½ x 10 ¾ INCHES

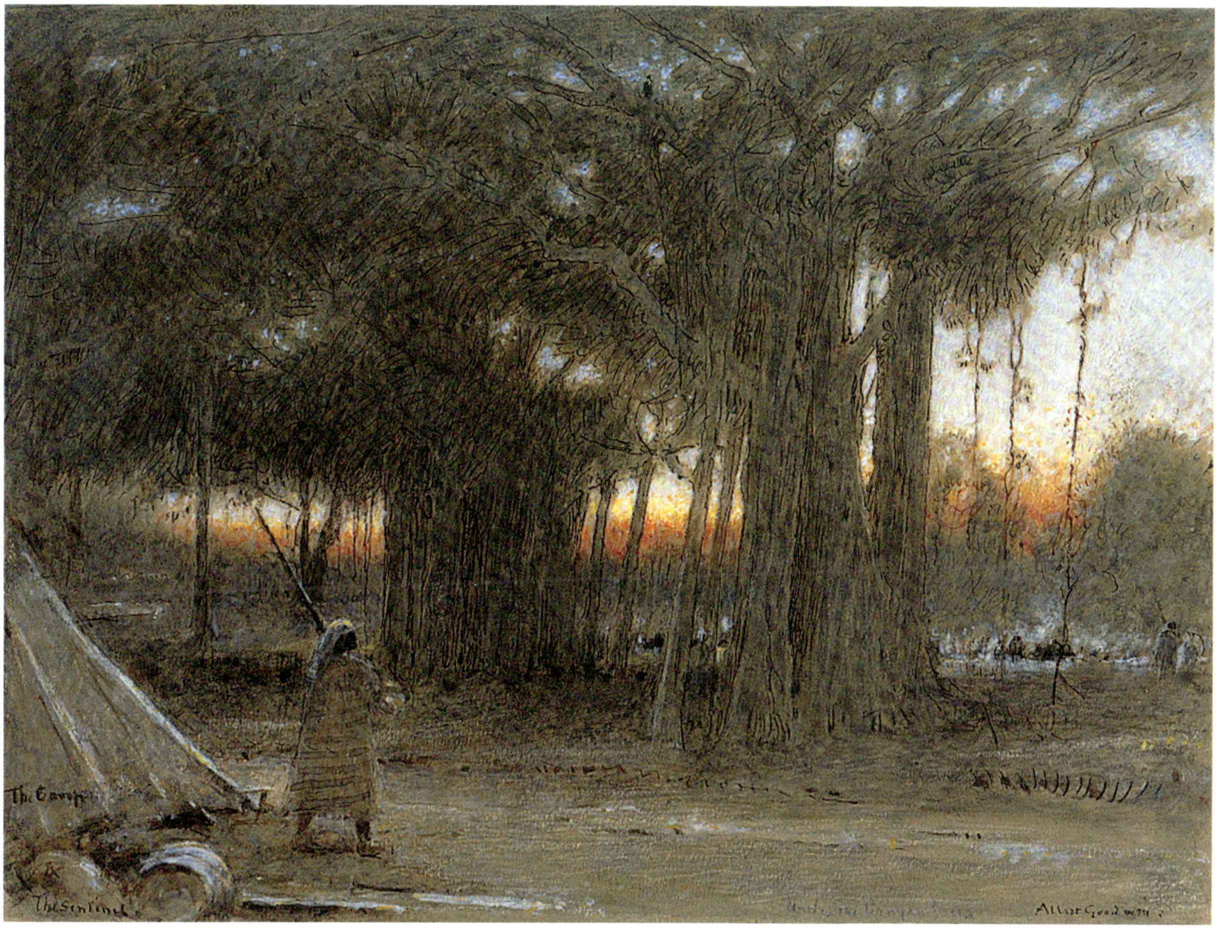

85 THE BANYAN TREES AND THE SENTINEL

signed, inscribed with title and 'Under the Banyan Trees'

watercolour, bodycolour and pen and ink on tinted paper

11 x 14 ¾ INCHES

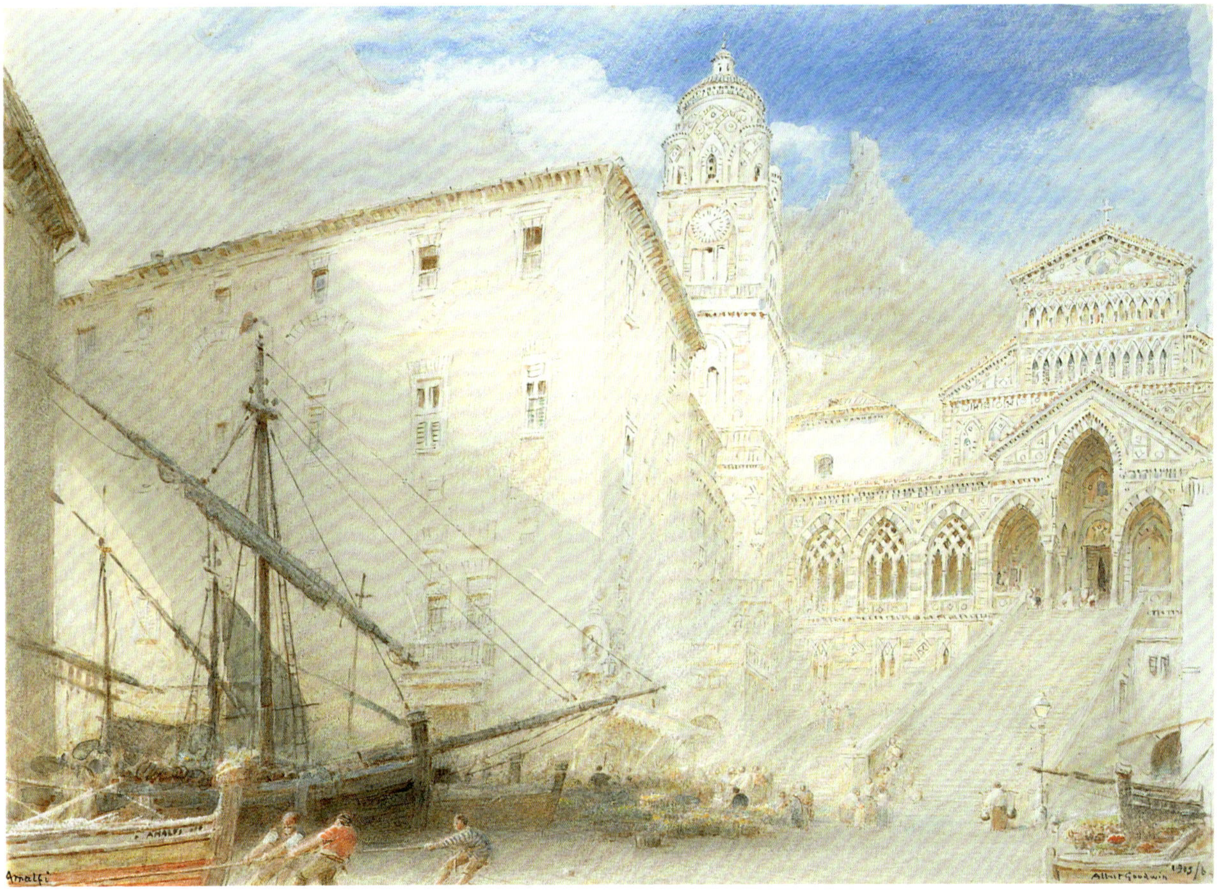

86 AMALFI

signed, inscribed with title and dated 1905/6
signed and inscribed with artist's address on a label on reverse of backboard
watercolour with pen and ink
11 x 15 INCHES

EXHIBITED: The Royal Society of Painters in Water-Colours, Summer 1906, no 237

87 NAPLES

signed and inscribed with title

pencil and bodycolour
on tinted paper

12 x 14 inches

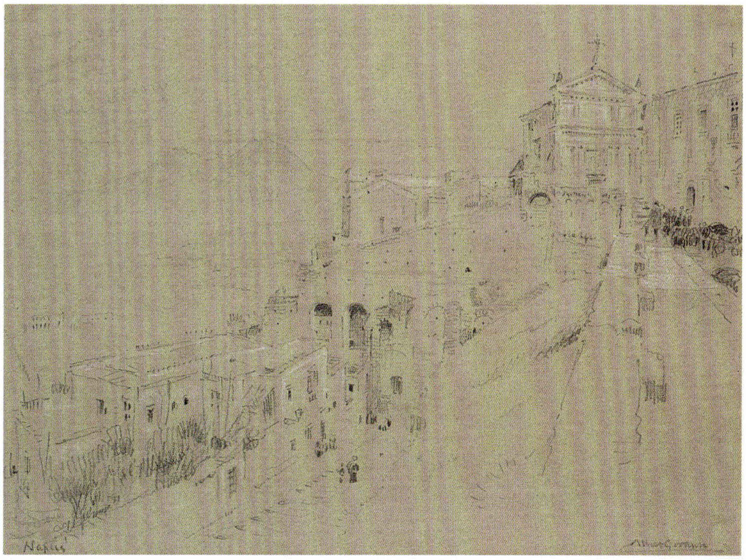

88 NAPLES

signed, inscribed with title and dated 1905

watercolour

10 ¼ x 14 ½ inches

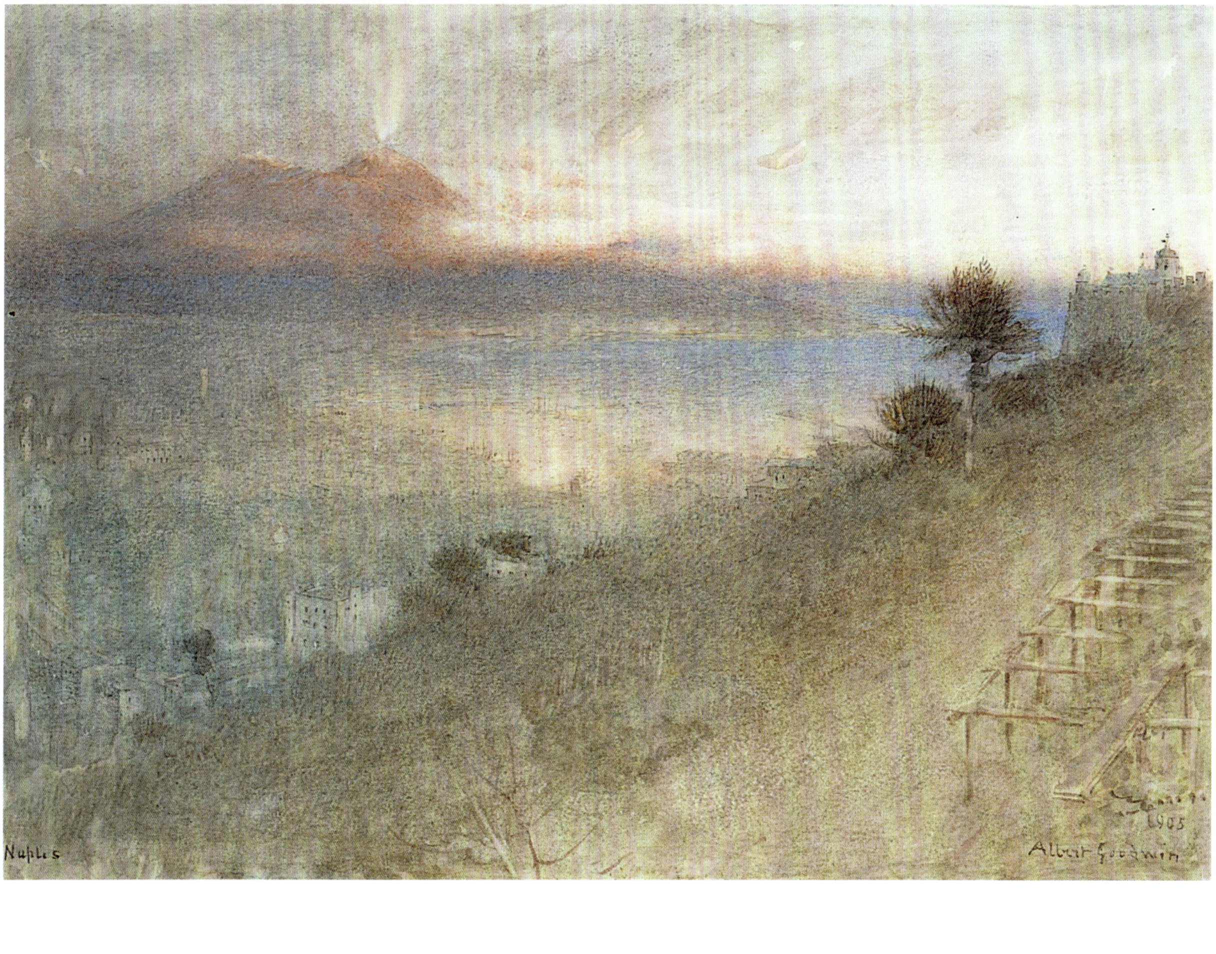

89 BERWICK ON TWEED

signed and inscribed with title

pen and ink and pencil

10 ½ x 15 INCHES

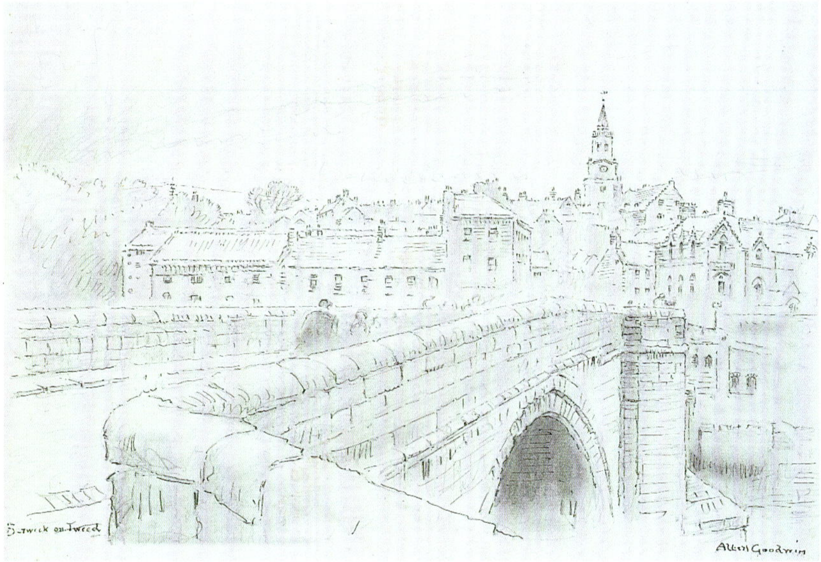

90 ELY

signed and inscribed with title

watercolour

10 x 14 INCHES

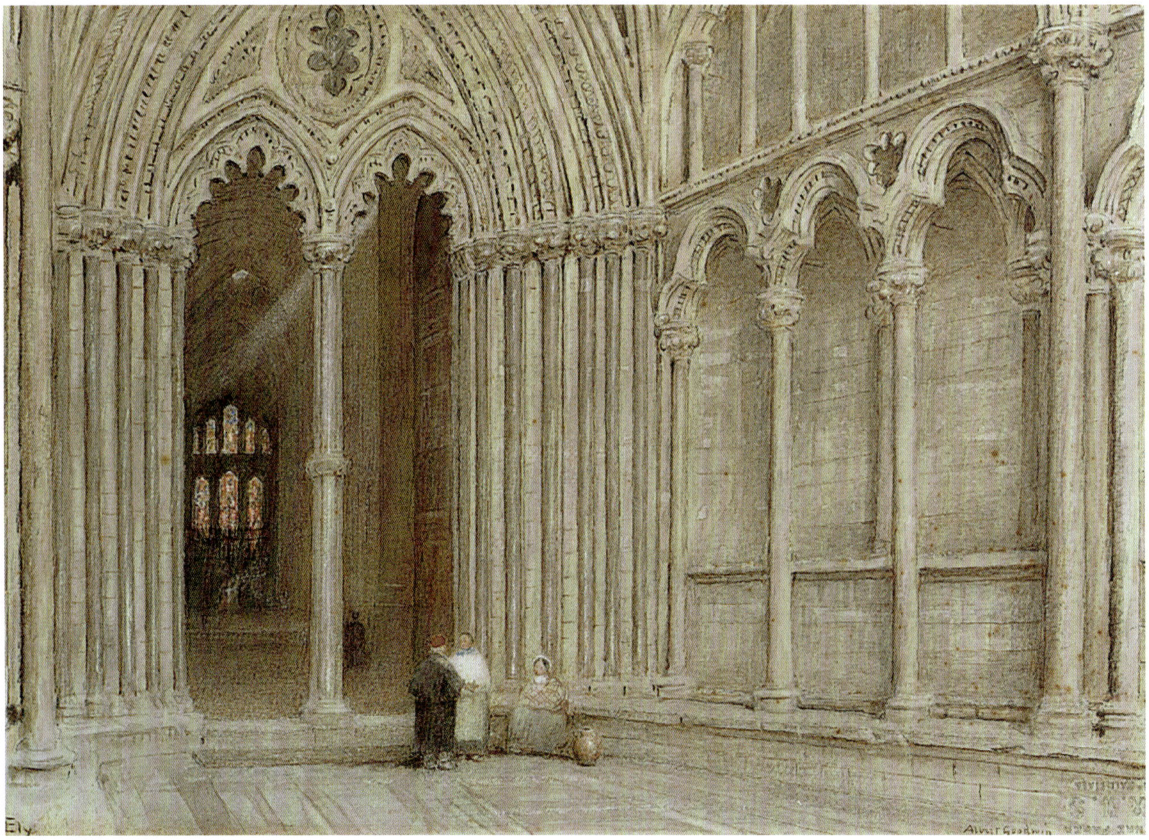

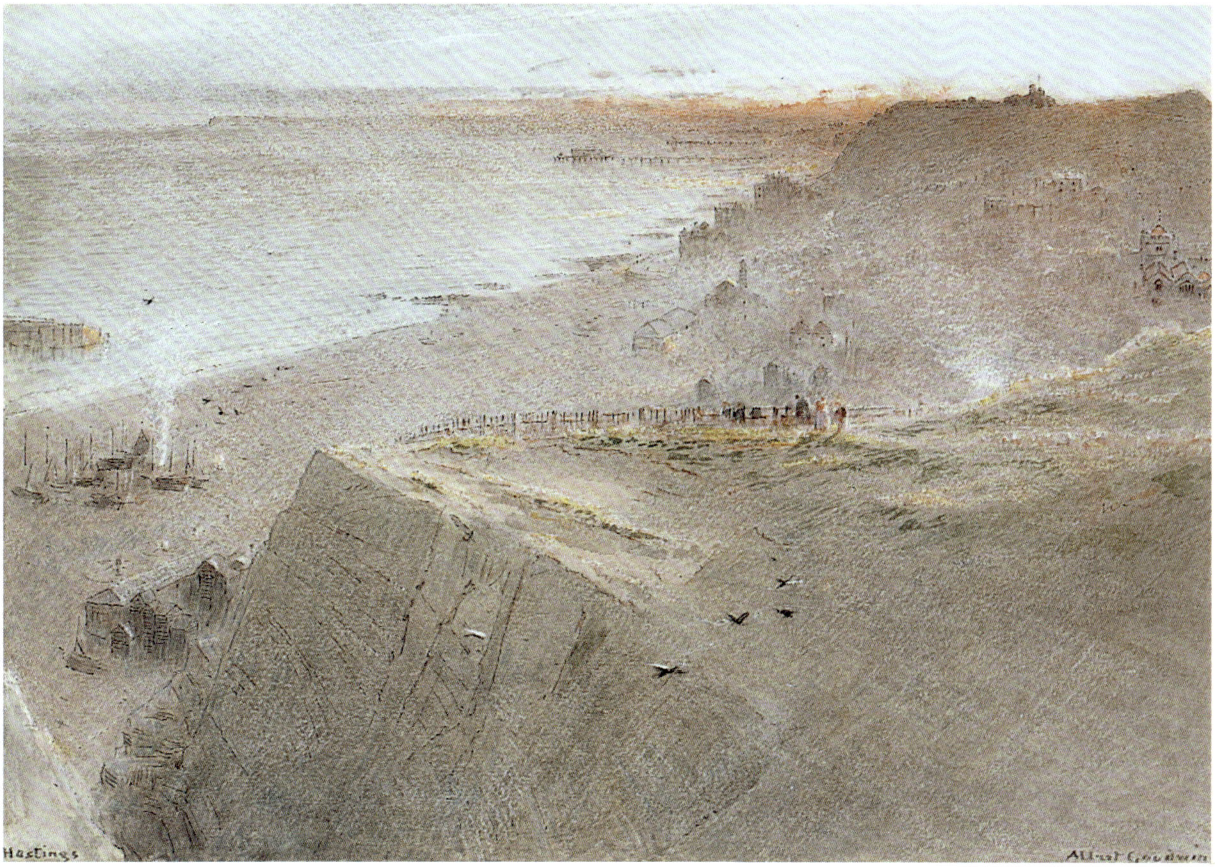

91 HASTINGS

signed and inscribed with title

watercolour

10 ½ x 14 ¾ INCHES

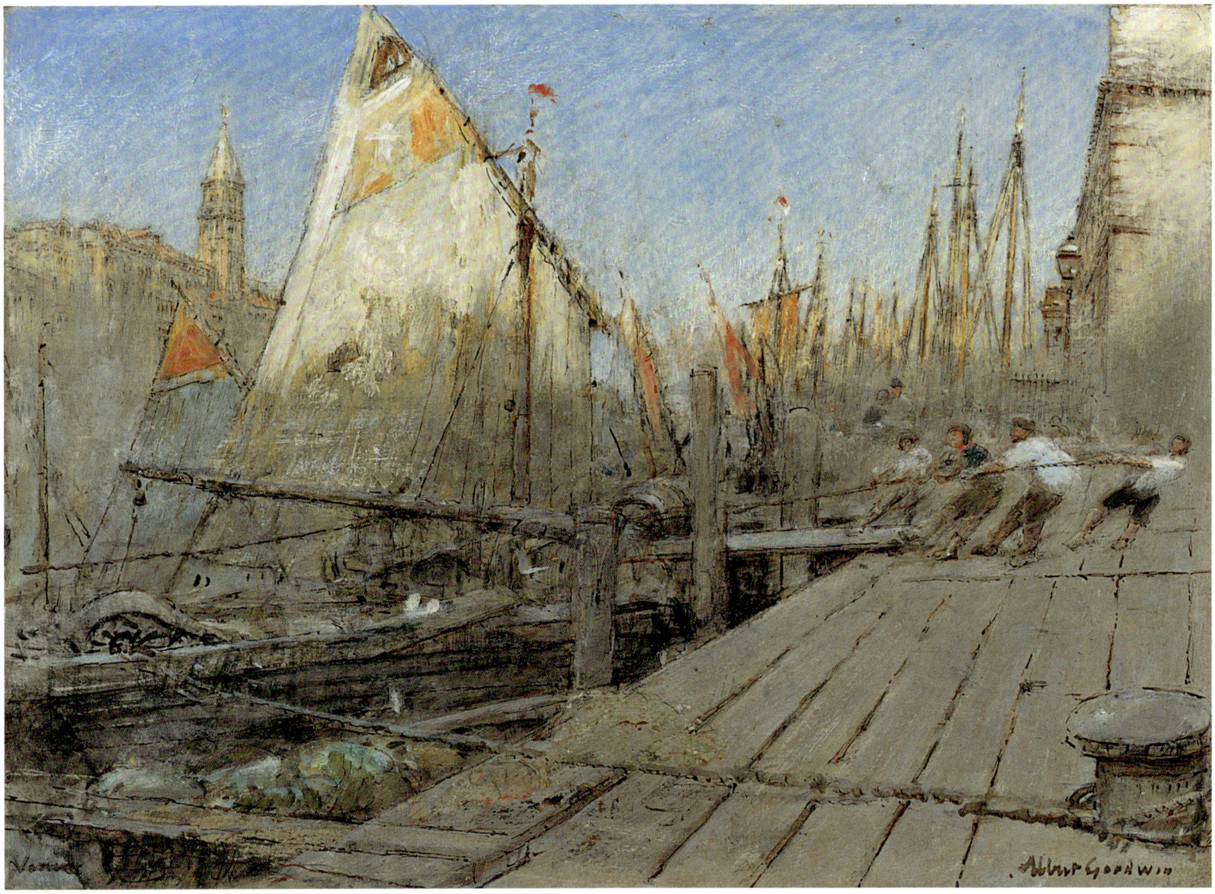

92 VENICE

signed and inscribed with title

oil on paper with decorative border

11 ½ x 15 ¾ INCHES

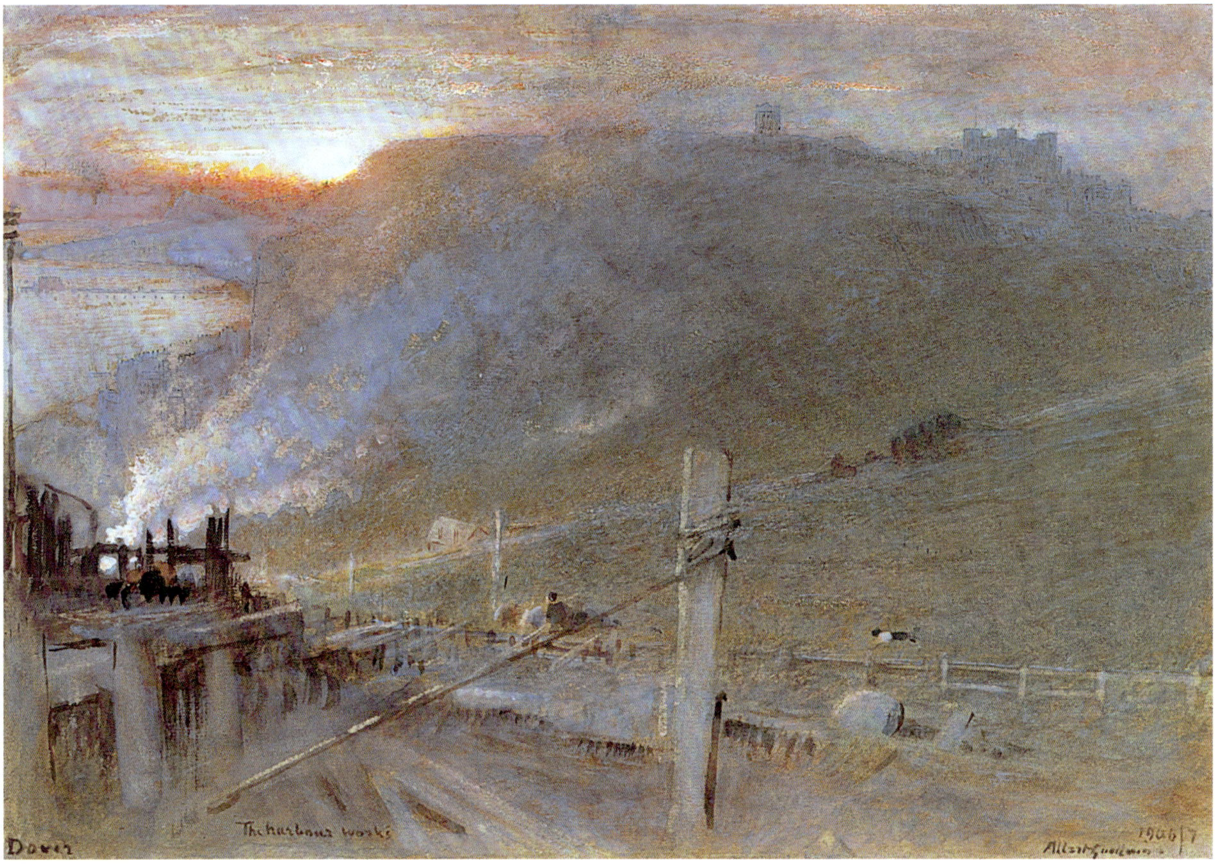

93 DOVER,
THE HARBOUR WORKS

signed, inscribed with title and dated 1906/7
watercolour with bodycolour
10 x 14 ½ INCHES

LITERATURE: *Albert Goodwin RWS 1845-1932*, London: Chris Beetles, 1986, plate 100, limited edition of 1000

EXHIBITED: 'Albert Goodwin, RWS 1845-1932', Touring Exhibition, May-October 1986, no 68

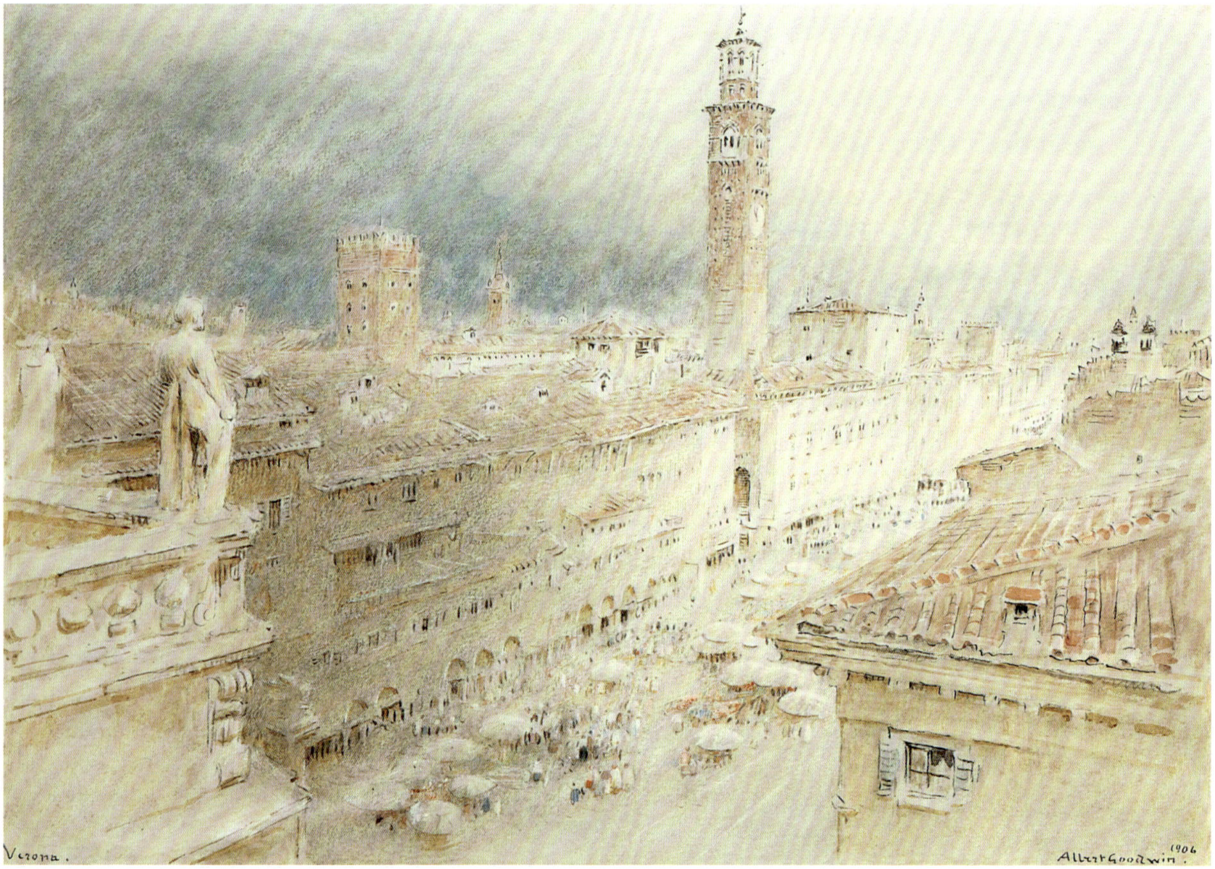

94 VERONA

signed, inscribed with title and dated 1906
watercolour
9 ½ x 13 ¼ INCHES

EXHIBITED: 'Albert Goodwin, RWS 1845-1932', Touring Exhibition, May-October 1986, no 105

A painting entitled 'Verona Market' was exhibited in 'Drawings and Pictures by Albert Goodwin, RWS', Leggatt Brothers Gallery, London, 1908, no 57

'...the Market Place at Verona! That wonderful medley of umbrellas, with the fruit-sellers and market-women, the splendid white oxon which came in from the country with farm produce; and over all the huge great Clock Tower, surely the most wonderful market-place the world has!'

Albert Goodwin, *Diary*, 1915

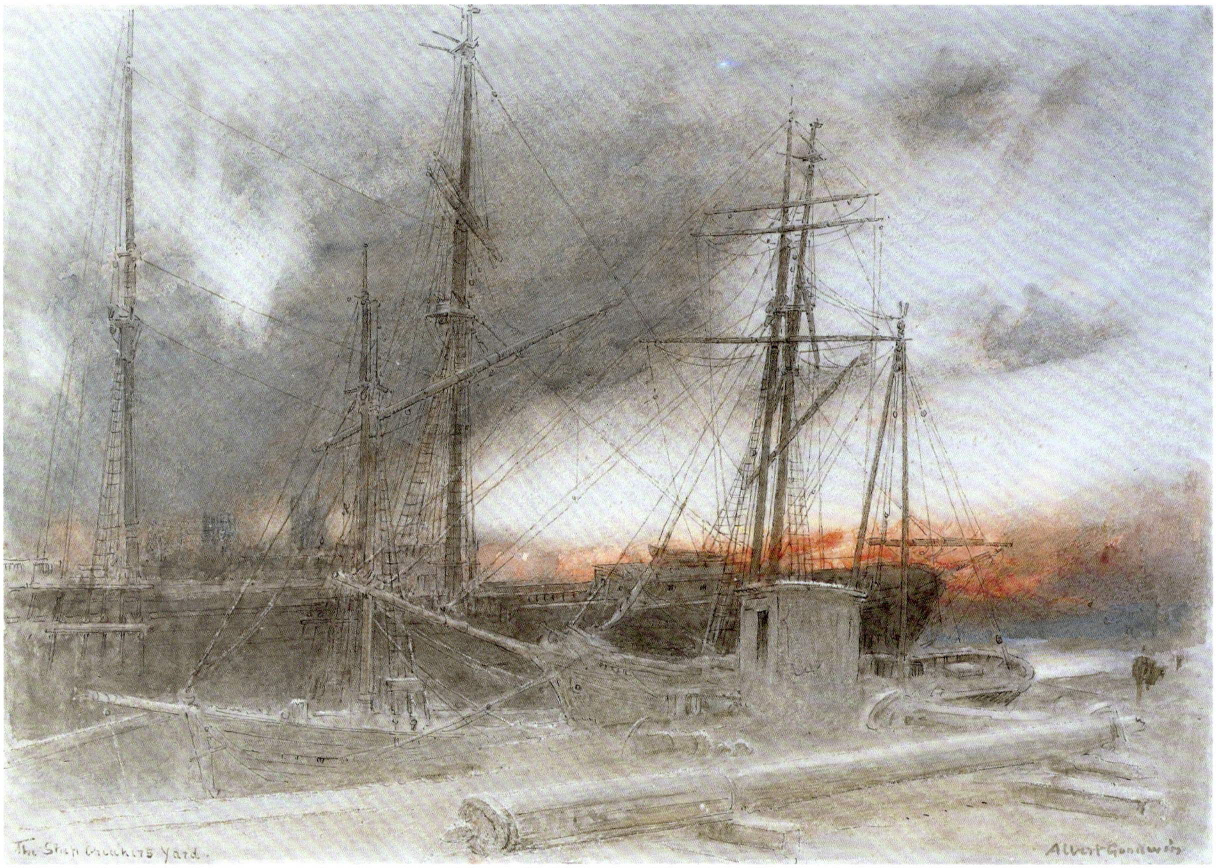

95 THE SHIPBREAKERS YARD (front endpapers)

signed and inscribed with title
watercolour with pen and ink
10 x 14 ½ INCHES

A painting of this title was exhibited in 'An Exhibition Of Watercolours of Dawn and Sunset', Fine Art Society, January 1907, no 32

not illustrated
96 THE BOATBUILDERS YARD
signed with initials
pencil with white crayon
6 ½ x 10 ½ INCHES

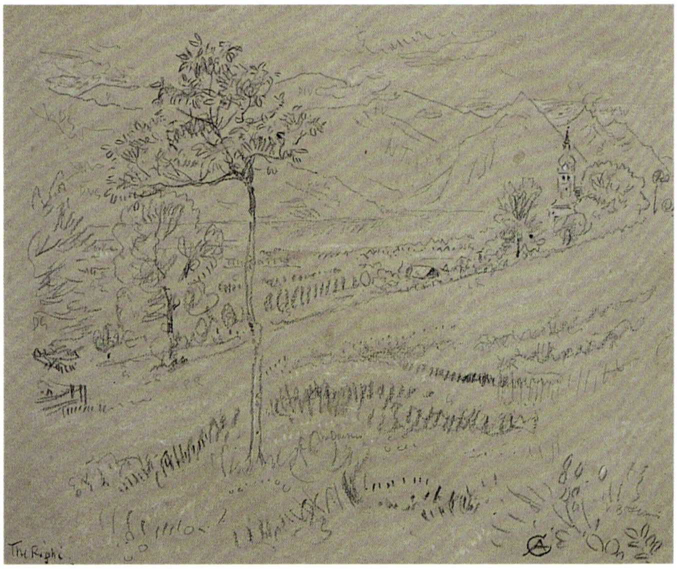

97 THE RIGHI

signed with monogram and inscribed with title

pencil on tinted paper

8 ¾ x 10 ¾ INCHES

98 BERNE

signed and inscribed with title

watercolour with pen and ink

10 x 14 INCHES

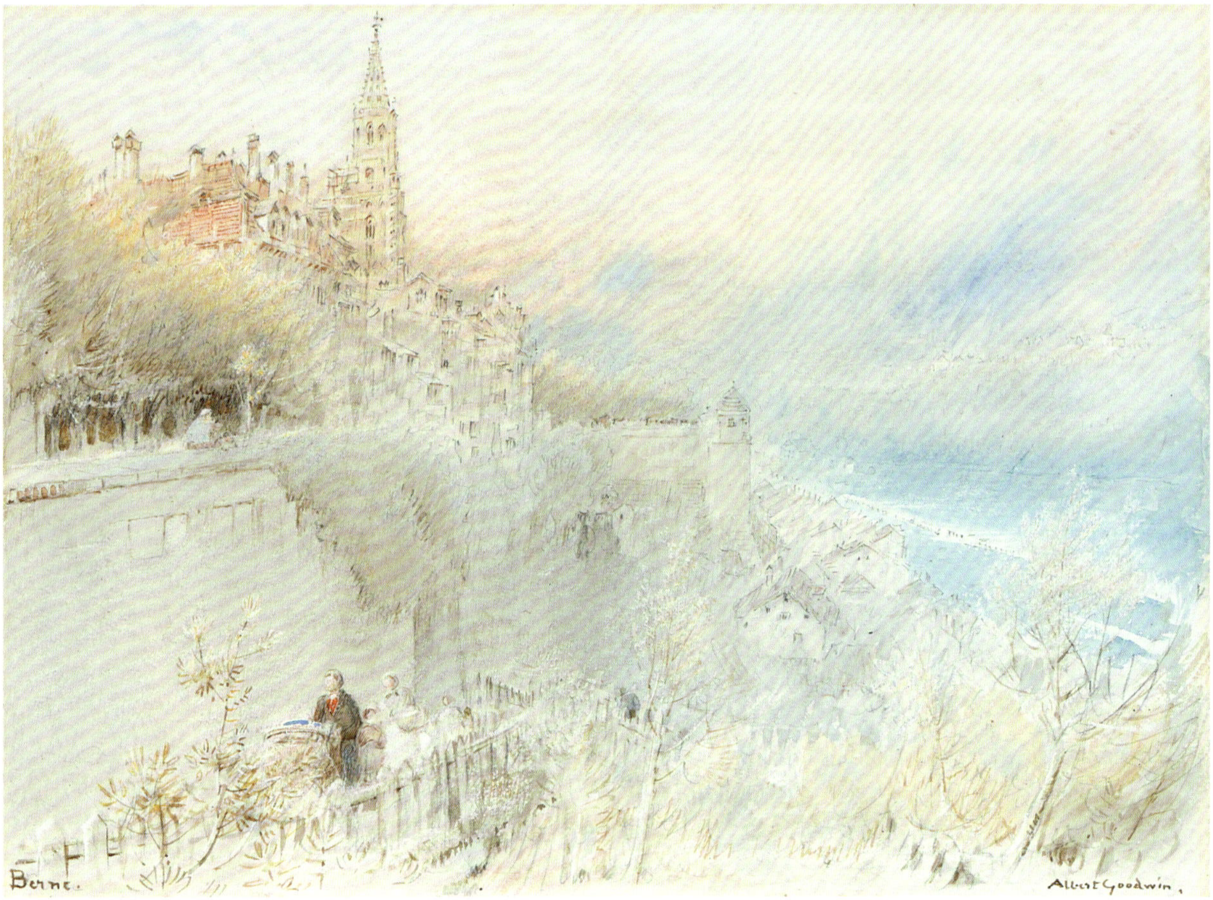

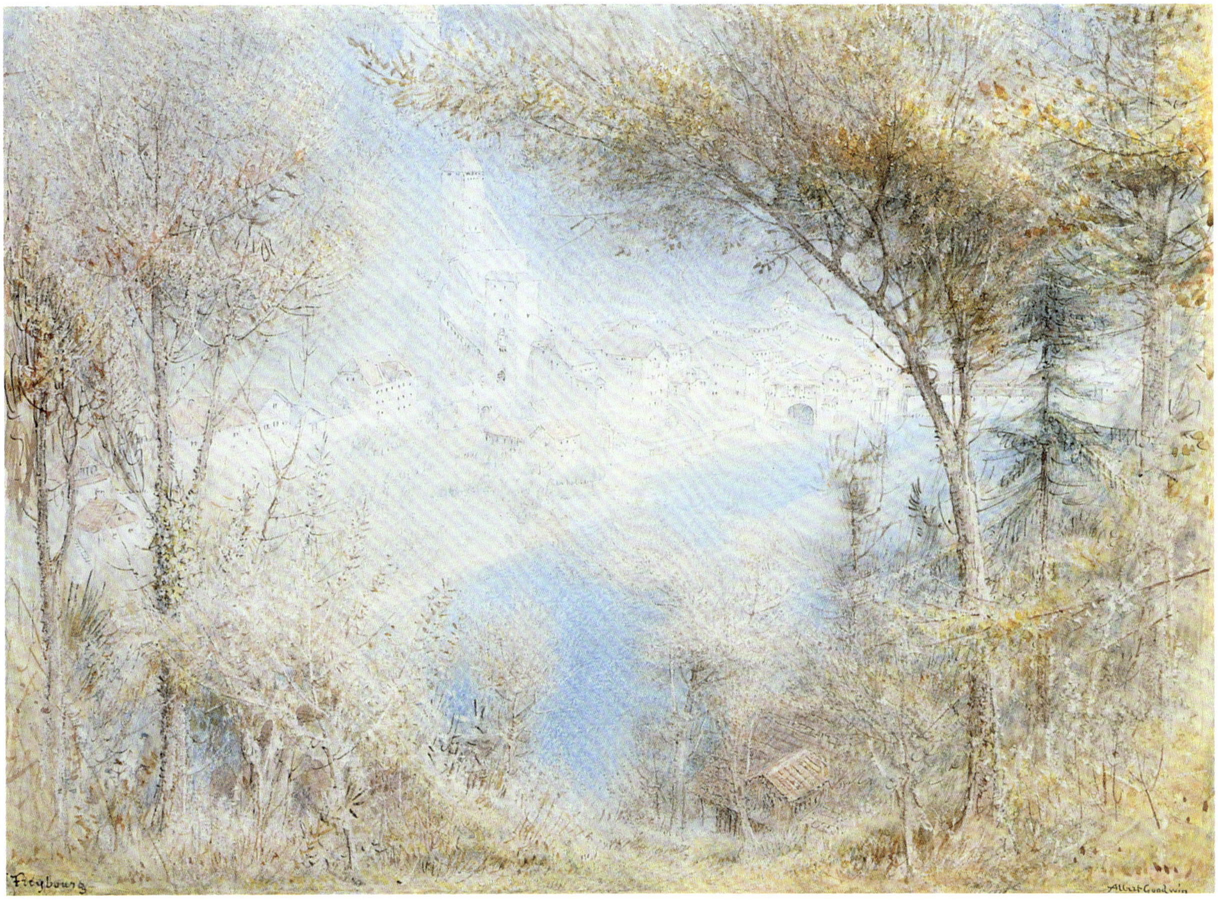

99 FREYBOURG
signed and inscribed with title
watercolour with pen and ink
10 x 14 ¼ INCHES

100 OXFORD – ORIEL COLLEGE
signed and inscribed with title
watercolour and bodycolour on tinted paper
10 x 14 INCHES

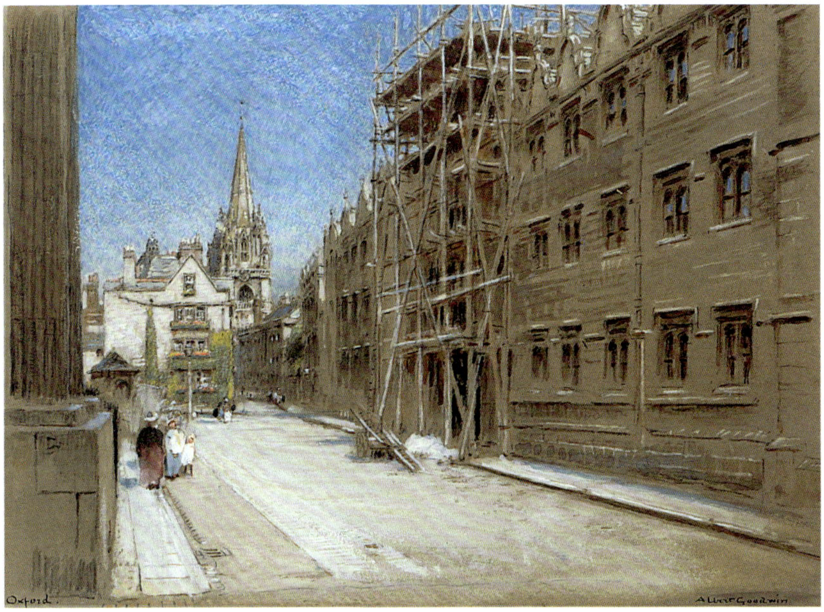

not illustrated
101 FRIBOURG (SUISSE)
signed, inscribed with title and dated 1910
watercolour and bodycolour with pen and ink
10 x 14 INCHES

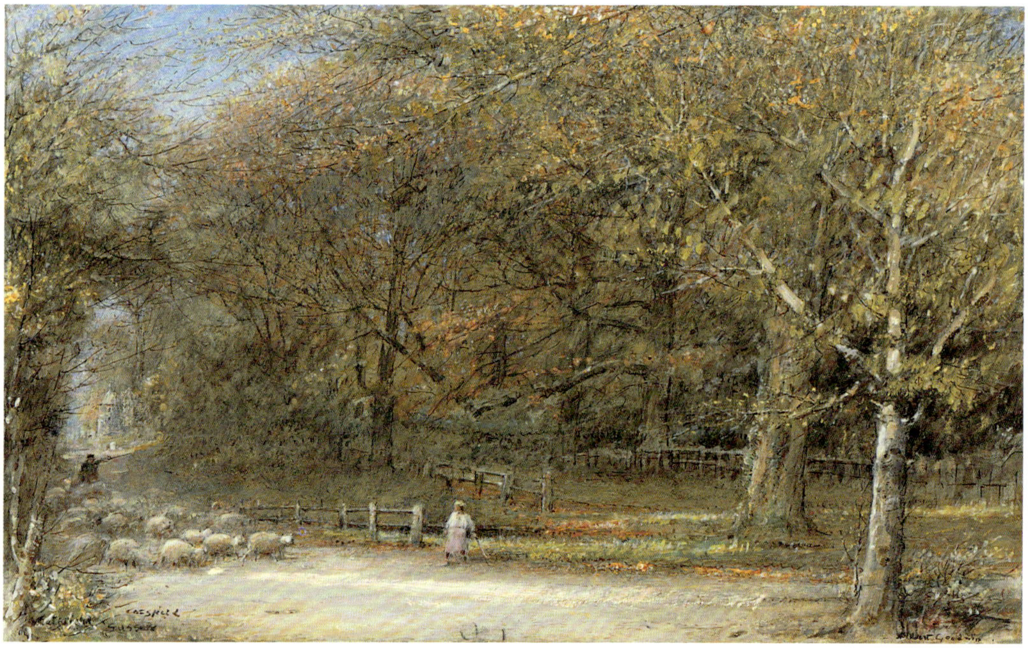

102 CATSFIELD, SUSSEX

signed and inscribed with title

pen and ink, watercolour and bodycolour

12 ½ x 20 INCHES

103 OLD INTERLAKEN

signed and inscribed with title

oil and watercolour with pen and ink

9 ½ x 14 ½ INCHES

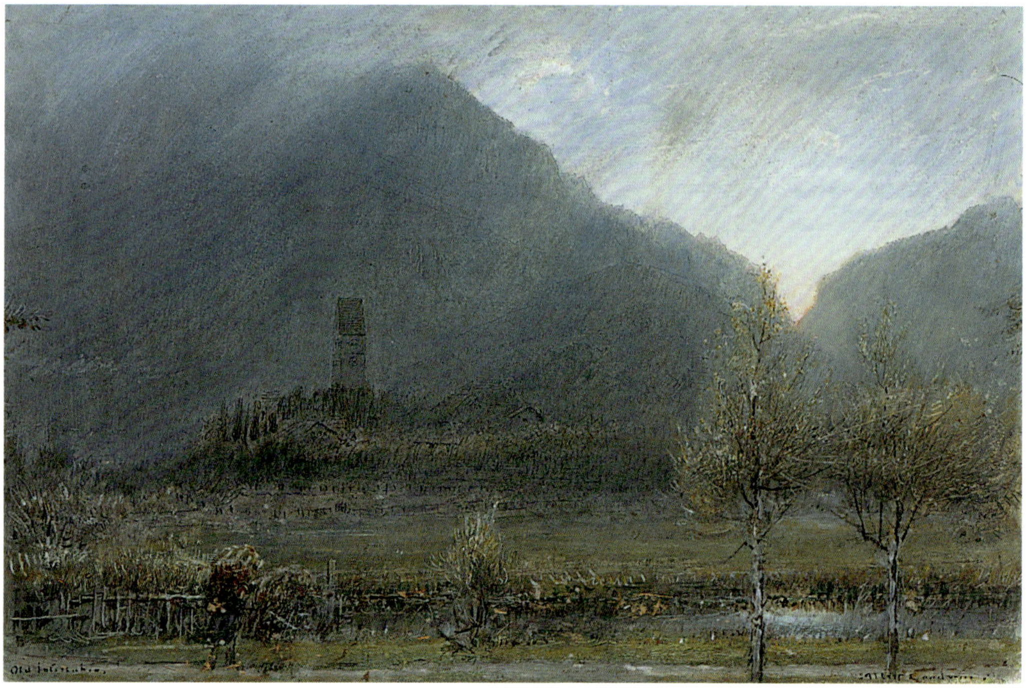

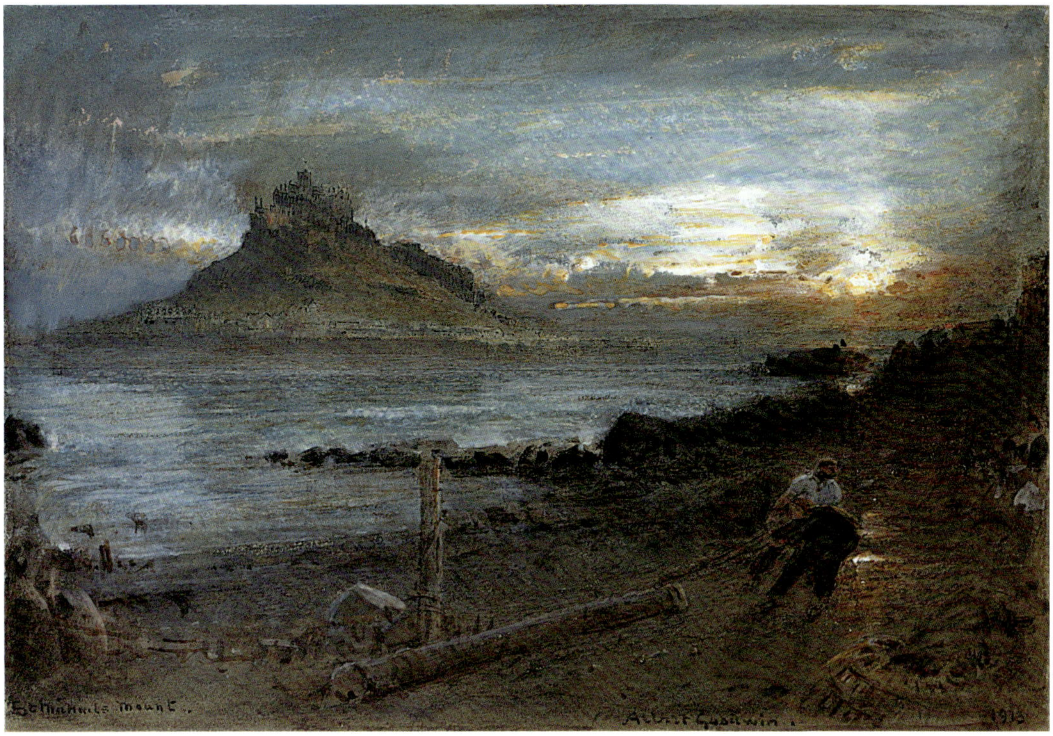

104 ST MICHAEL'S MOUNT

signed, inscribed with title and dated 1913
watercolour and bodycolour on tinted paper
10 x 14 ¾ INCHES

A painting of this title was exhibited at the Royal Society of Painters in Water-Colours, Summer 1914, no 135

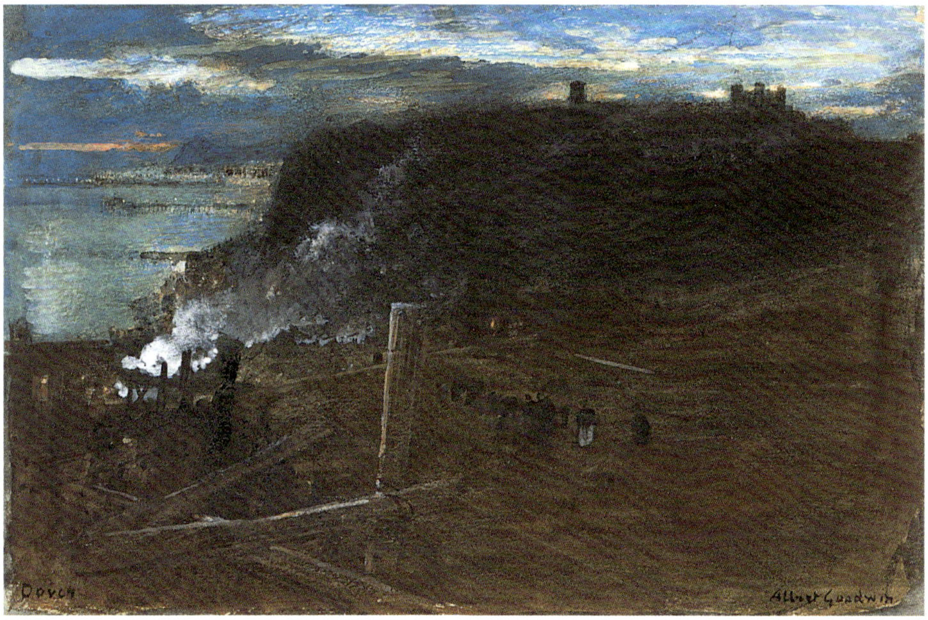

105 DOVER

signed and inscribed with title
watercolour with bodycolour on tinted paper
5 ¼ x 8 ½ INCHES

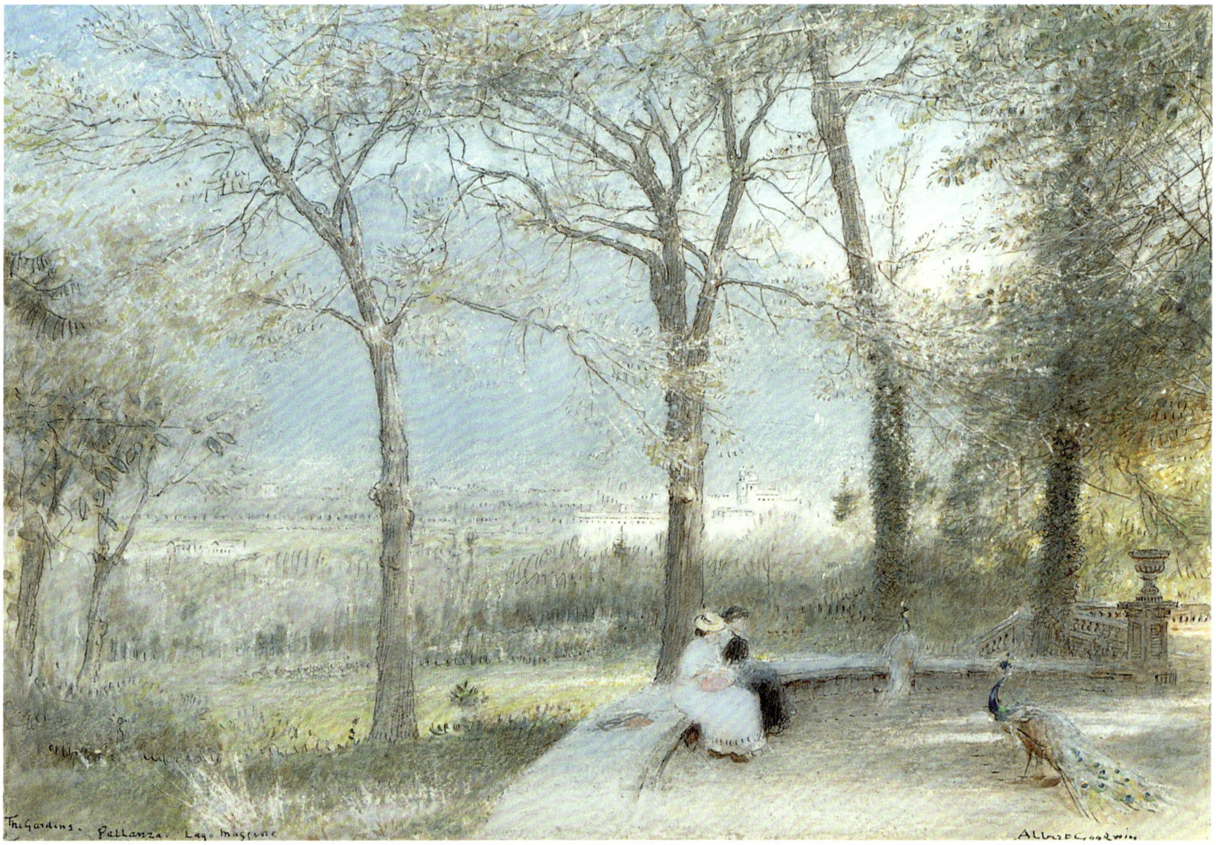

106 THE GARDENS, PALLANZA, LAGO MAGGIORE

signed and inscribed with title
watercolour with pen and ink
and bodycolour
10 x 14 ¾ INCHES

EXHIBITED: Royal Society of Painters
in Water-Colours, Winter 1915, no 2

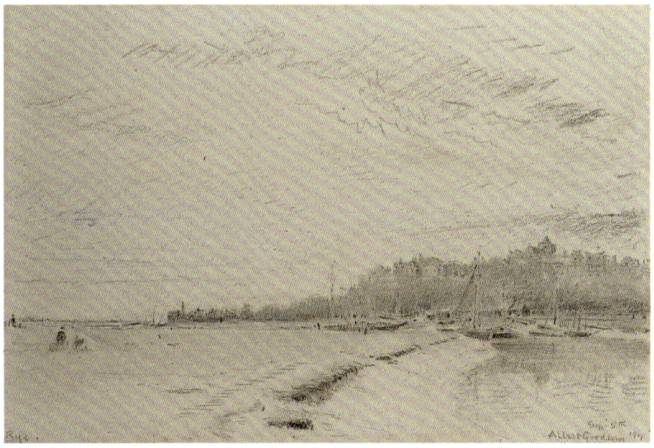

108 RYE

signed, inscribed with title
and dated 'Sept 5th '97'
pencil and charcoal
9 ½ x 14 INCHES

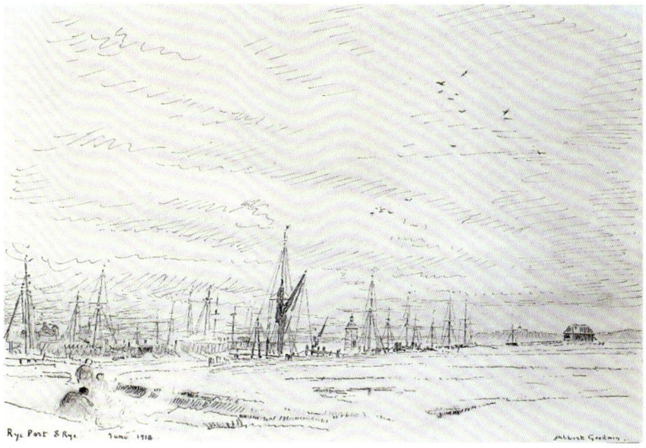

109 RYE PORT & RYE

signed, inscribed with title
and dated 'June 1918'
pen and ink with pencil
10 x 13 ¾ INCHES

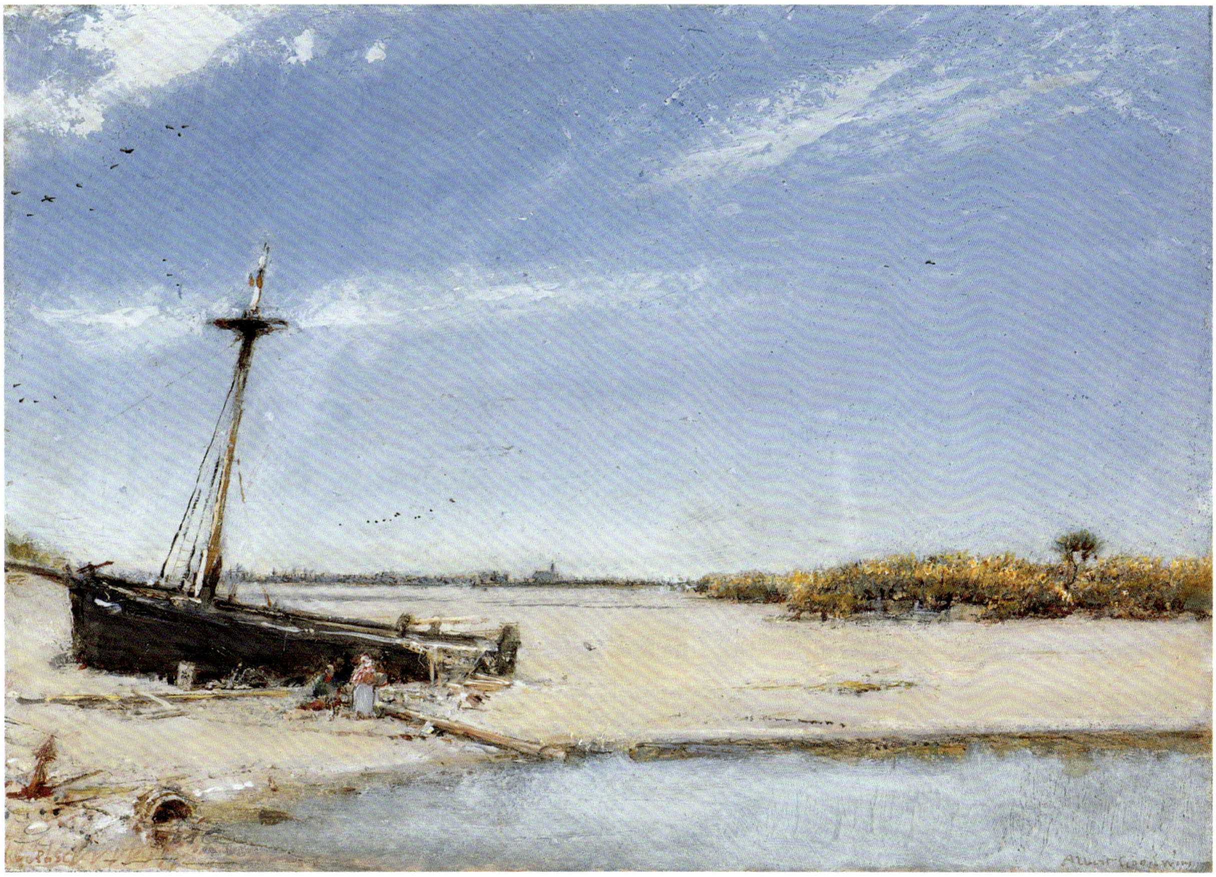

107 RYE PORT

signed and inscribed with title
watercolour and bodycolour
9 ½ x 13 ¼ INCHES

ILLUSTRATED: Hammond Smith, *Albert Goodwin RWS*, Leigh-on-Sea: F Lewis, 1977, plate 4

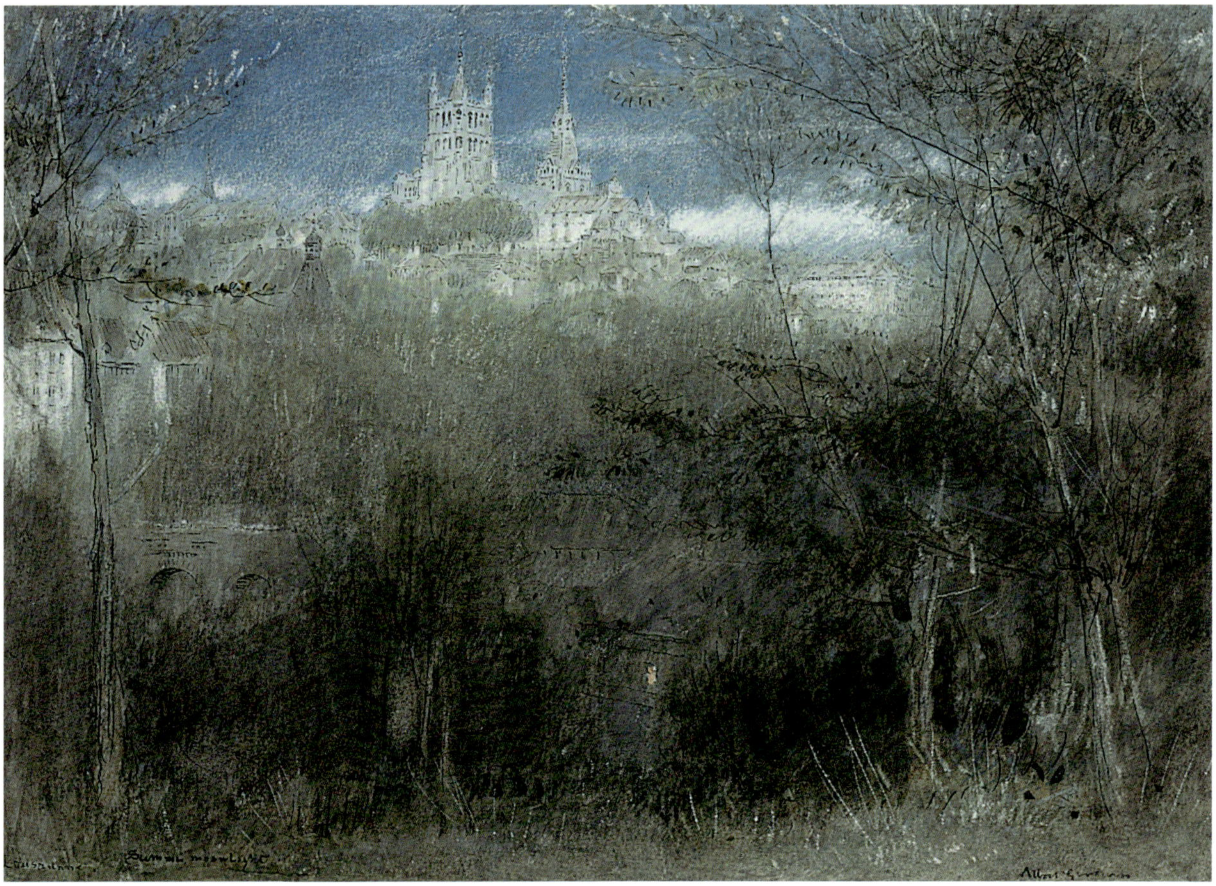

110 LAUSANNE, SUMMER MOONLIGHT

signed and inscribed with title

watercolour and bodycolour with pen and ink

10 x 14 ½ INCHES

EXHIBITED: 'Albert Goodwin, RWS 1845-1932', Touring Exhibition, May-October 1986, no 116

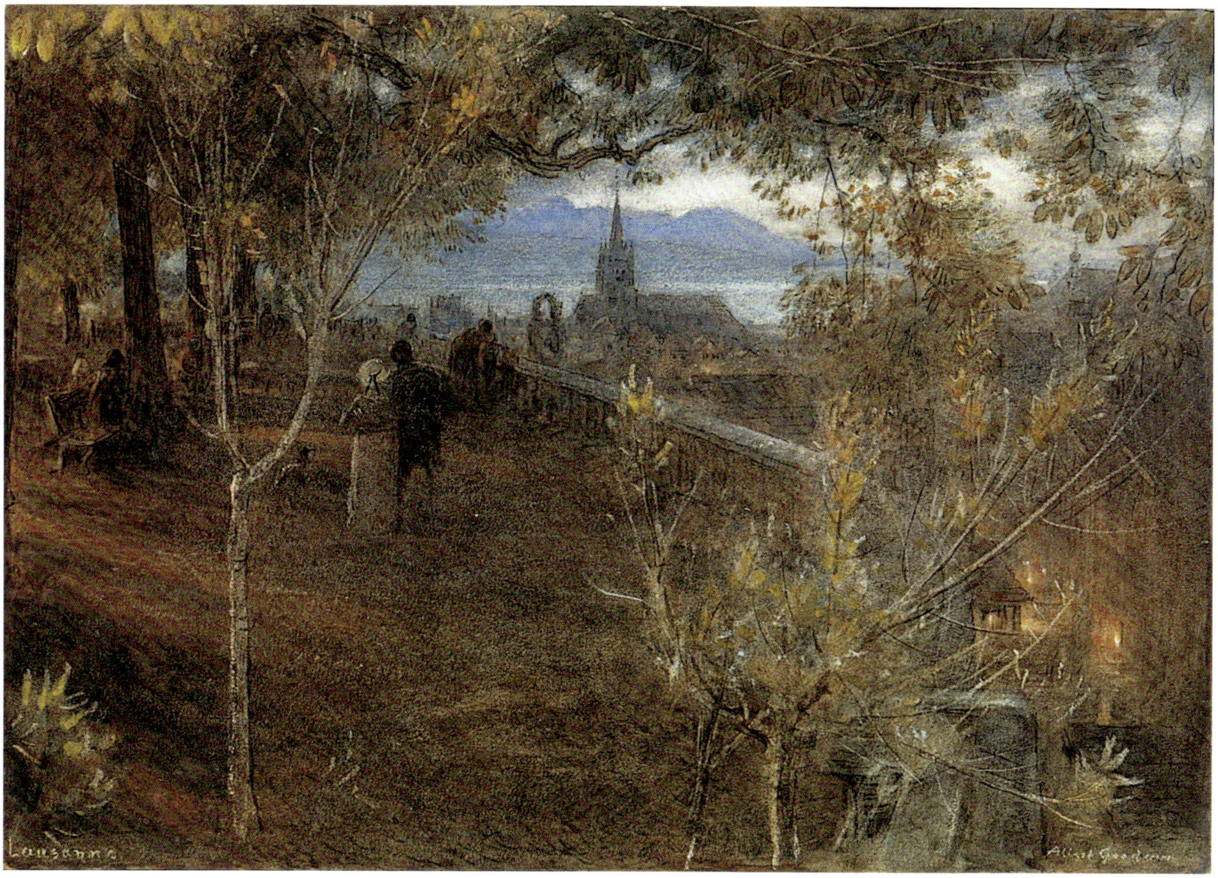

111 LAUSANNE

signed and inscribed with title
watercolour with bodycolour
10 ½ x 15 ¼ INCHES

A painting of this title was exhibited at the Royal Society of Painters in Water-Colours, Winter 1917, no 57

112 CHRISTCHURCH, HANTS

signed, inscribed with title and dated 1919
pen and ink and watercolour with bodycolour
10 x 14 INCHES

PROVENANCE:
Thomas Agnew and Sons;
Lord Croft

A painting of this title was exhibited at the Royal Society of Painters in Water-Colours, Winter 1921, no 270

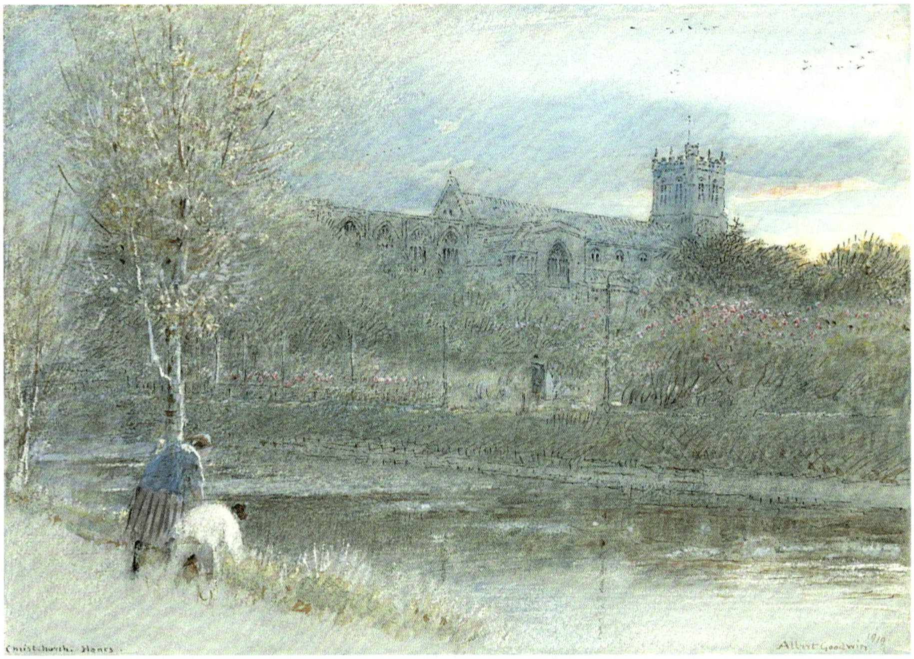

113 THE WRECK

signed, inscribed with title and indistinctly dated 19
watercolour with pen and ink
10 x 13 ¾ INCHES

EXHIBITED: the Royal Society of Painters in Water-Colours, Summer 1922, no 120

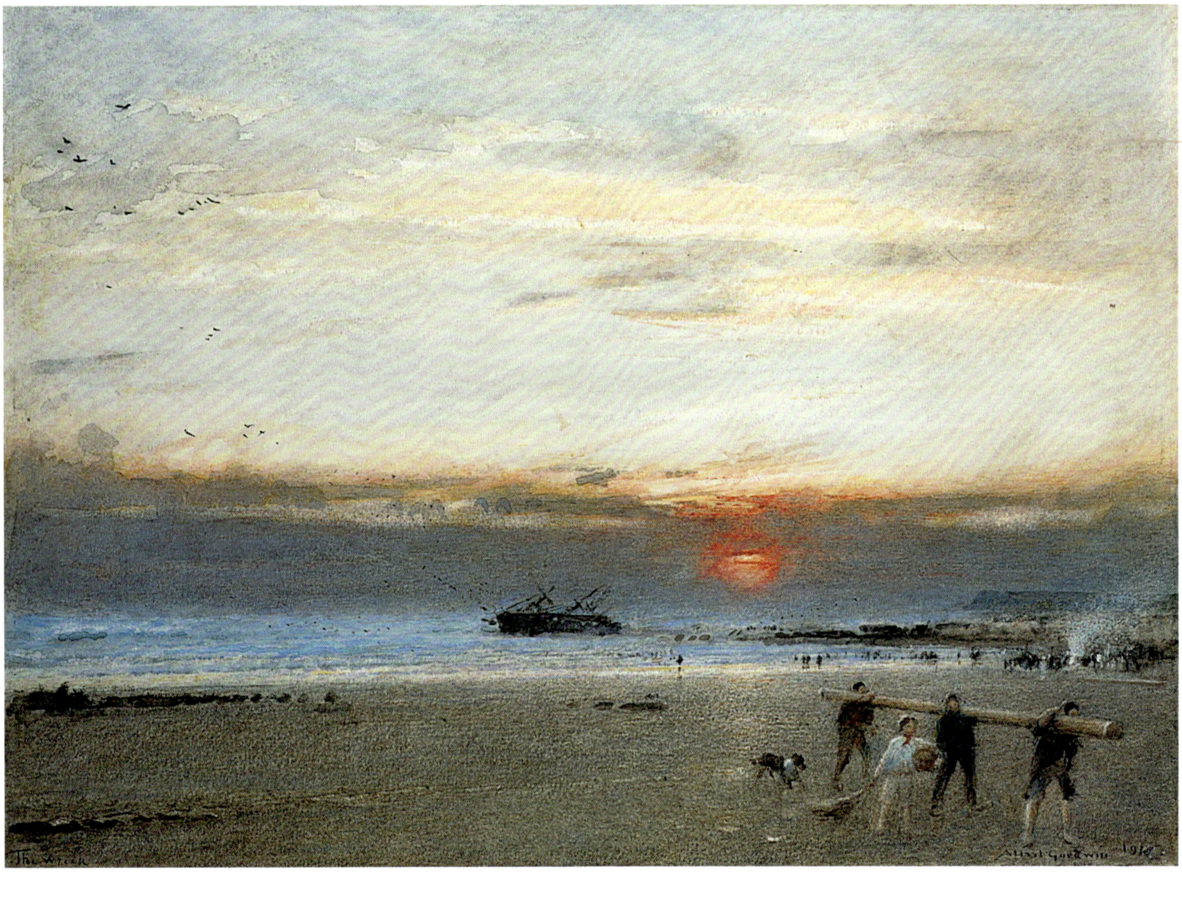

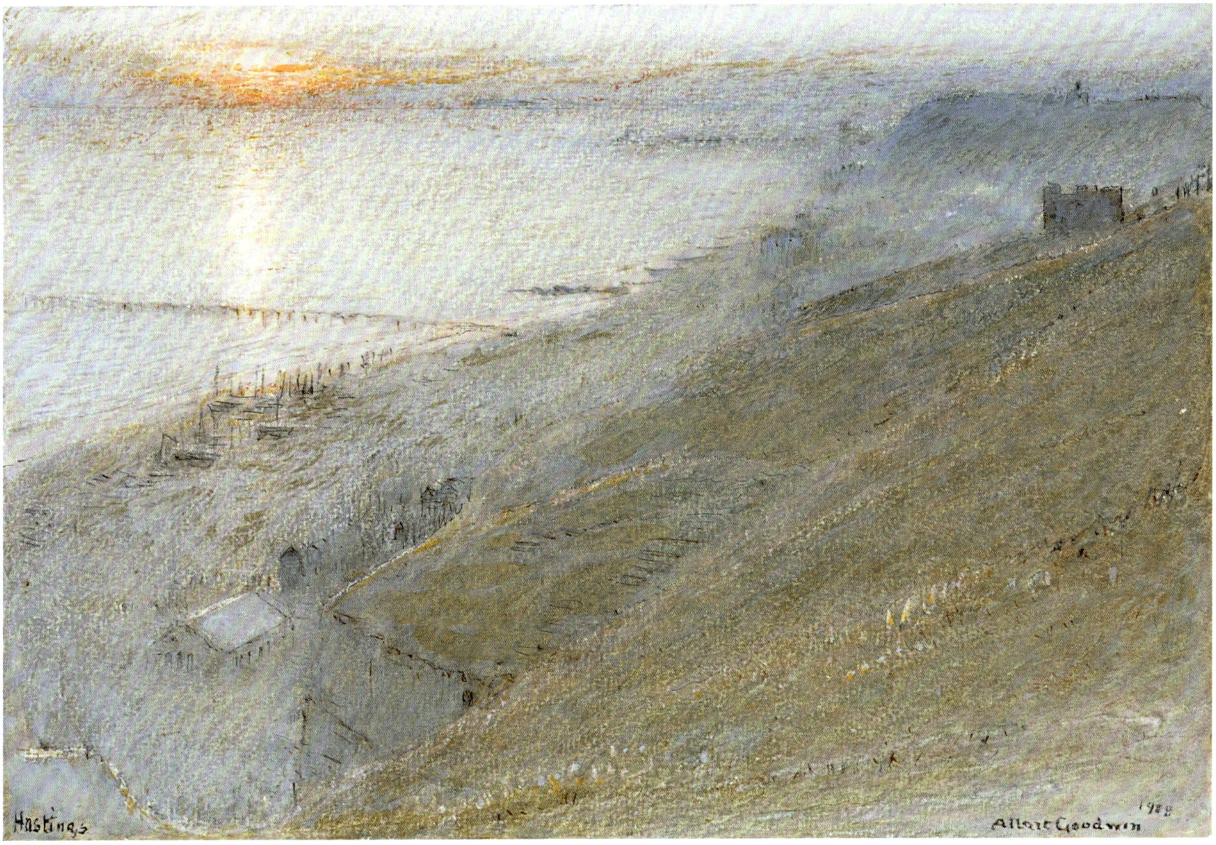

114 HASTINGS, WINTER SUNSET

signed, inscribed with title and dated 1918
watercolour with pen and ink
7 ½ x 10 ¾ INCHES

LITERATURE: *Albert Goodwin RWS 1845-1932*, London: Chris Beetles, 1986, plate 182, limited edition of 1000

EXHIBITED: 'Albert Goodwin, RWS 1845-1932', Touring Exhibition, May-October 1986, no 119

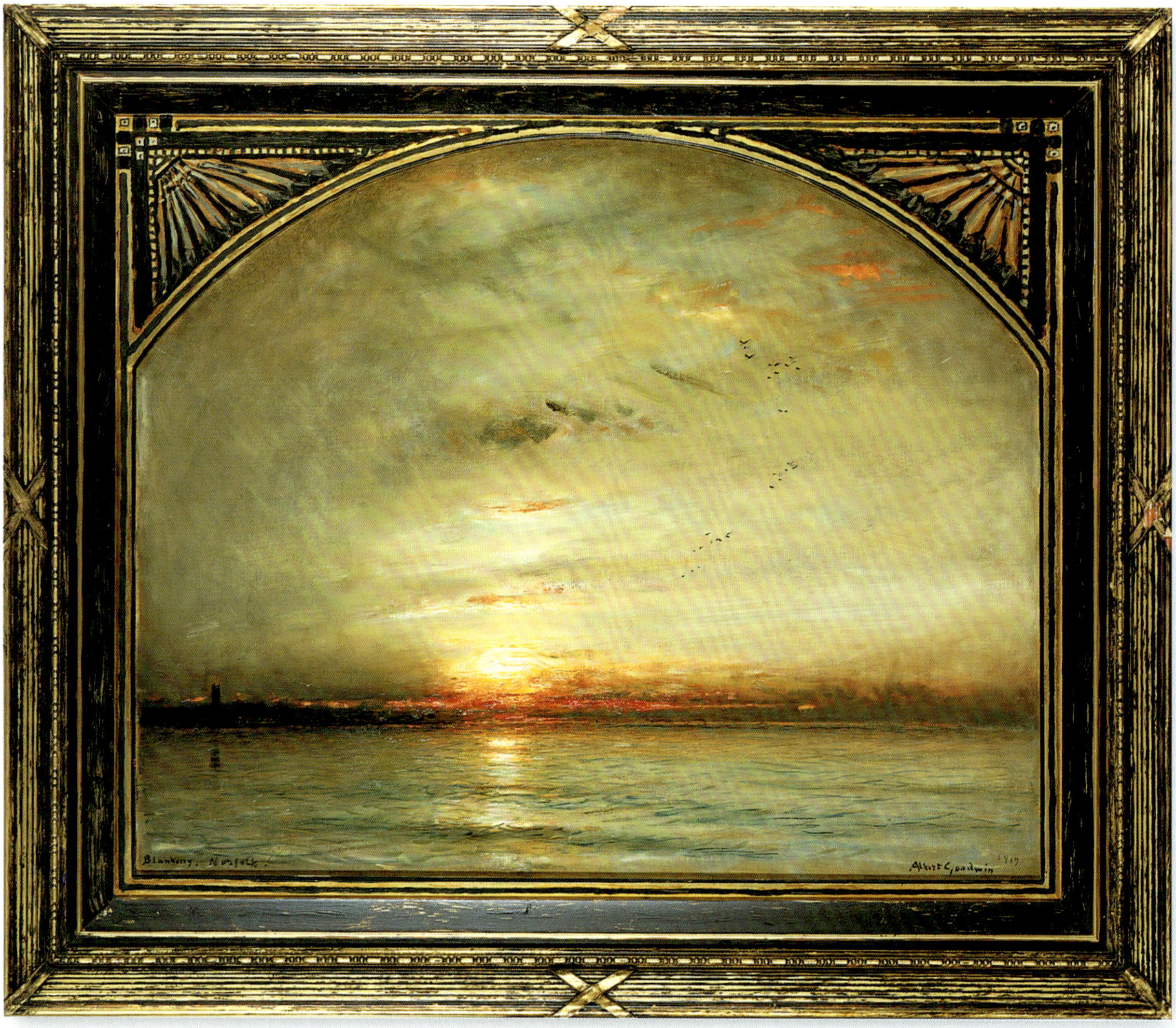

115 BLAKENEY NORFOLK (cover)

signed, inscribed 'Blankeny. Norfolk.' and dated 1919
oil on canvas
24 ¾ x 28 ¼ INCHES
In a gilded frame decorated by Albert Goodwin
measuring 33 ½ x 40 ½ INCHES

EXHIBITED: 'Albert Goodwin, RWS 1845-1932', Touring Exhibition, May-October 1986, no 105

'Nature is by no means uniform and perplexingly opposite to that hence its endless charm.'

Albert Goodwin, *Diary*

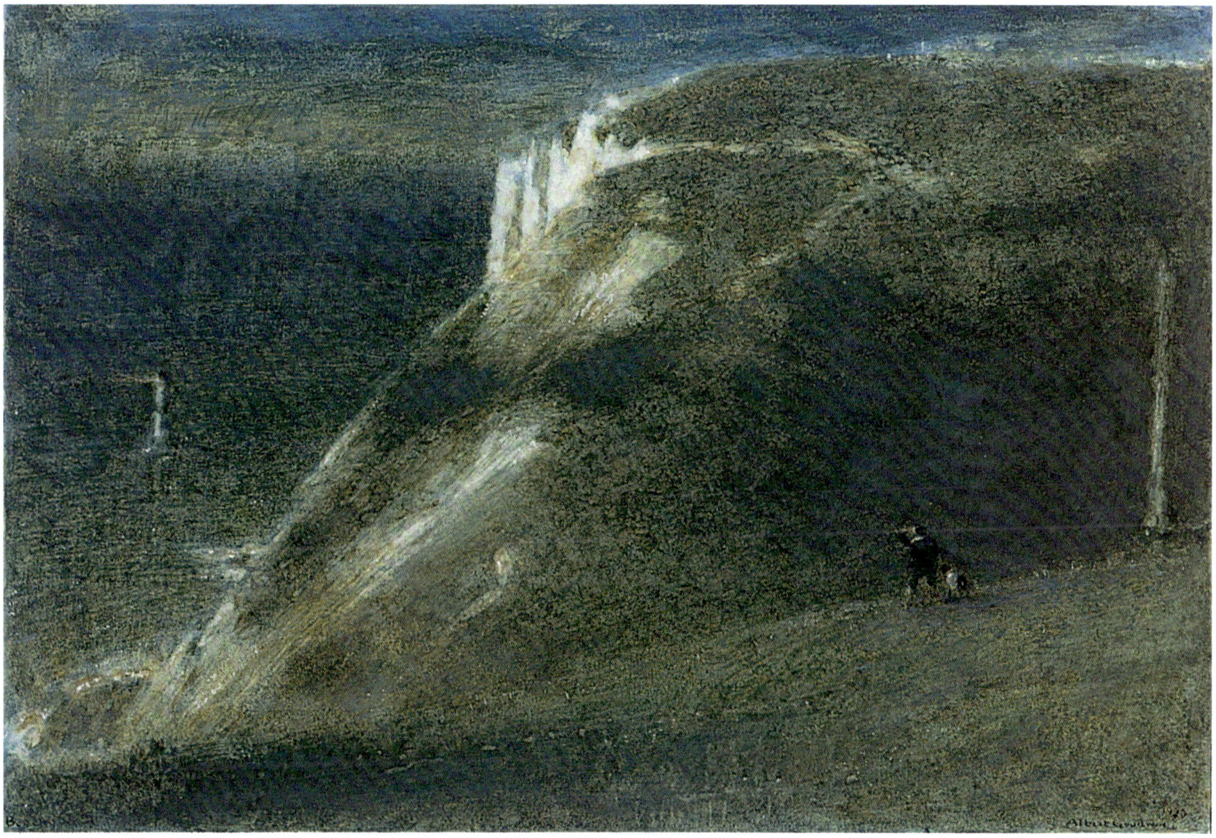

116 BEACHY HEAD

signed, inscribed with title and dated 1920
watercolour with bodycolour
13 ¾ x 20 ½ INCHES

EXHIBITED: Royal Society of Painters in Water-Colours, Summer 1920, no 148

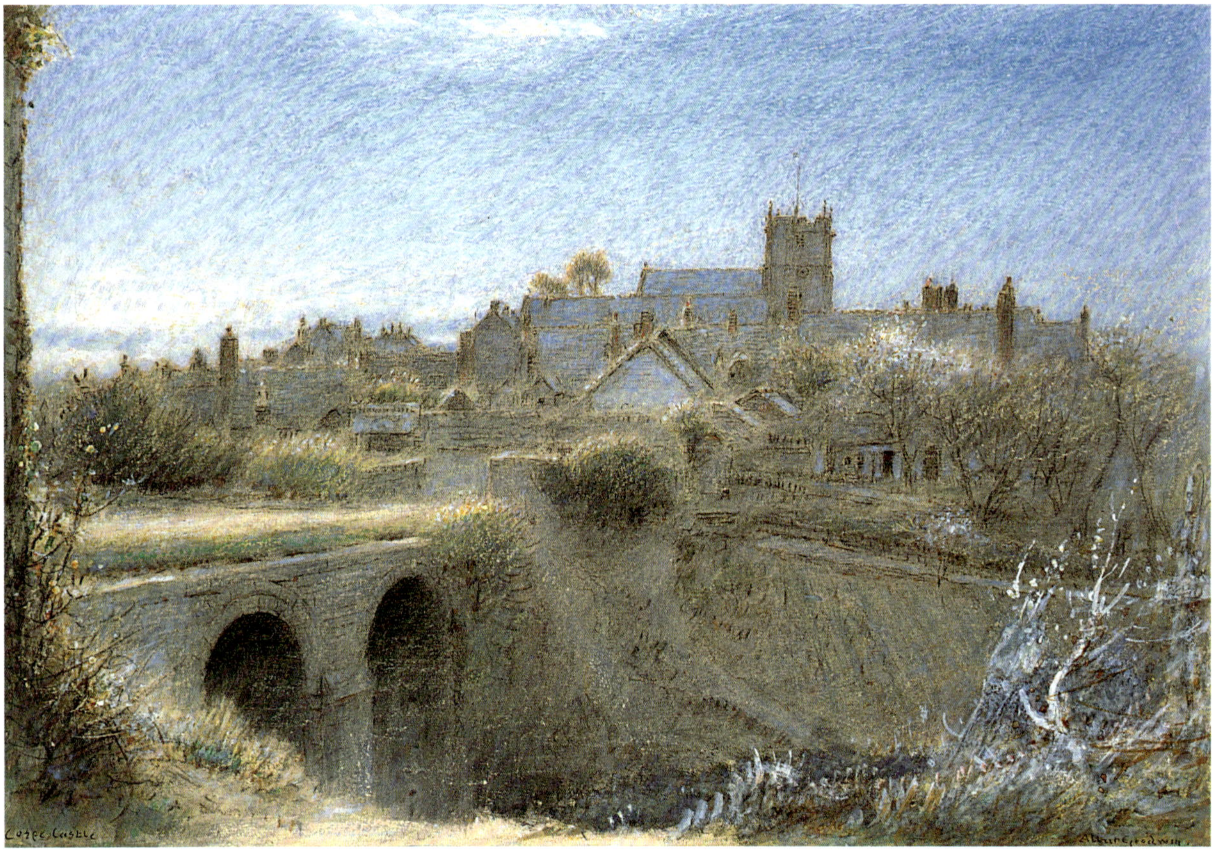

117 THE VILLAGE OF CORFE

signed and inscribed 'Corfe Castle'

watercolour, bodycolour and pencil

14 ¼ x 21 ¼ INCHES

LITERATURE: *Albert Goodwin RWS 1845-1932*, London: Chris Beetles, 1986, plate 108, limited edition of 1000

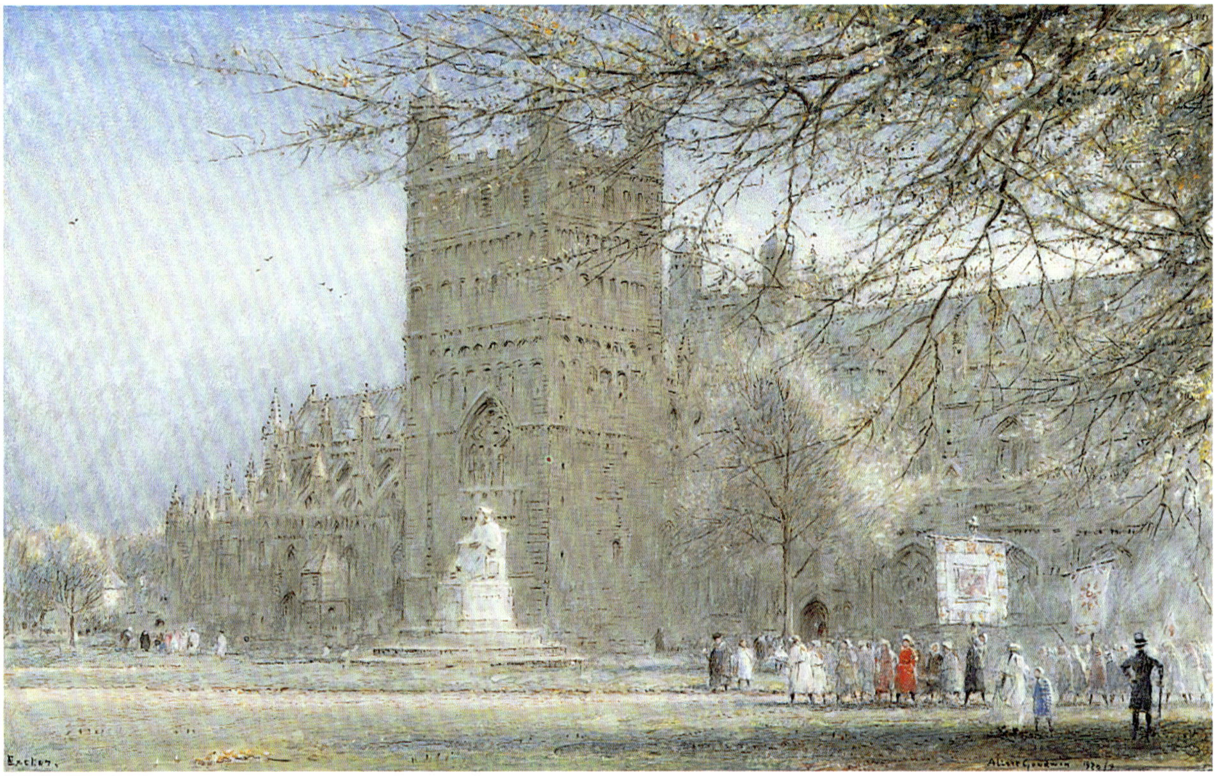

118 EXETER

signed, inscribed with title and dated 1920/4
watercolour, bodycolour and pen and ink
14 ½ x 23 INCHES

EXHIBITED: Royal Society of Painters
in Water-Colours, Summer 1924, no 69

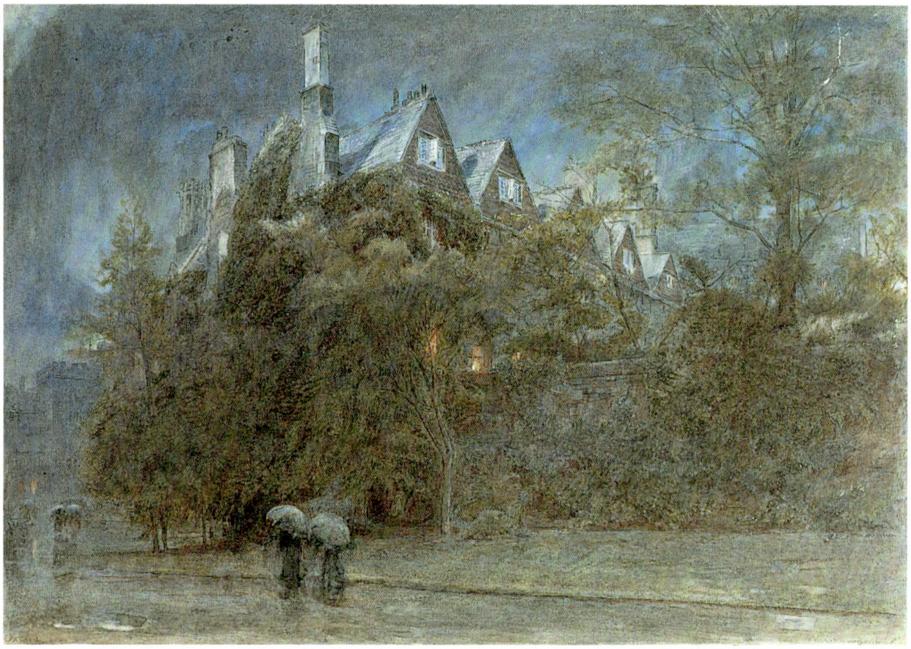

119 VIEW FROM THE ENTRANCE TO MEADOW BUILDING, CHRISTCHURCH COLLEGE, OXFORD

signed inscribed 'Oxford' and dated /23
watercolour with pen and ink
14 x 20 ¼ INCHES

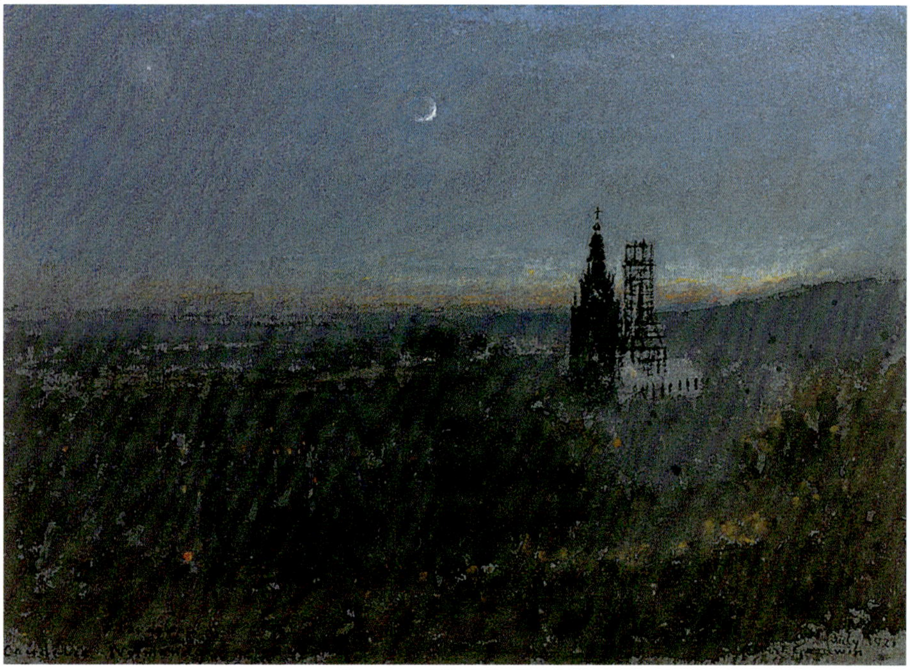

120 CAUDEBEC, NORMANDY

signed, inscribed with title and dated 'July 1921'
watercolour on tinted paper
10 x 13 ¾ INCHES

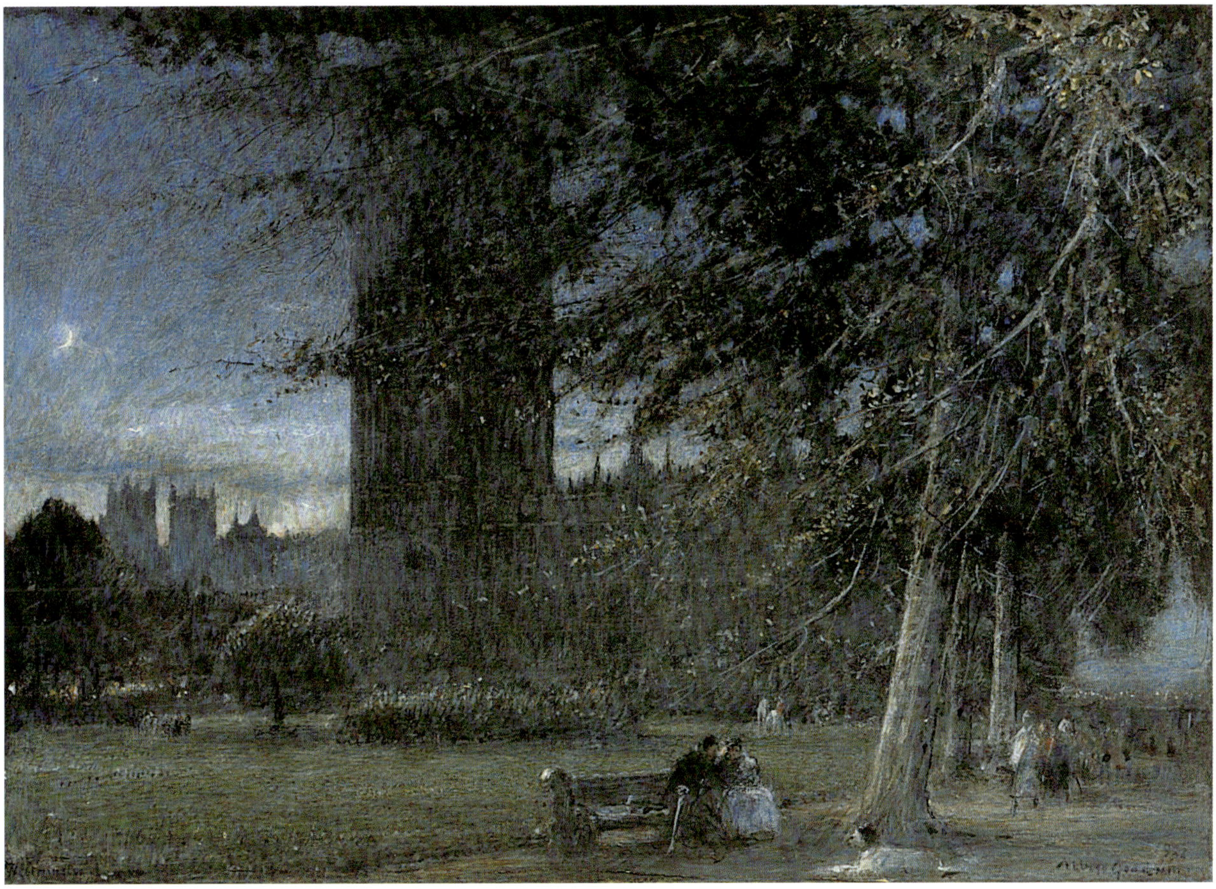

121 WESTMINSTER

signed, inscribed with title and dated 1922
watercolour with bodycolour
16 x 22 ½ INCHES

A painting of this title was exhibited in 'Water-Colour Drawings and Oil Paintings by Albert Goodwin, RWS', Vicars Brothers, London, March 1925, no 16

not illustrated

122 MONT ST MICHEL

signed and inscribed 'Mt St Michel'
watercolour and bodycolour
over a photographic base
9 x 11 INCHES

123 EXETER

signed, inscribed with title and dated 1922
watercolour with pencil and bodycolour
13 ½ x 21 INCHES

A painting of this title was exhibited at the Royal Society of Painters in Water-Colours, Summer 1924, no 69

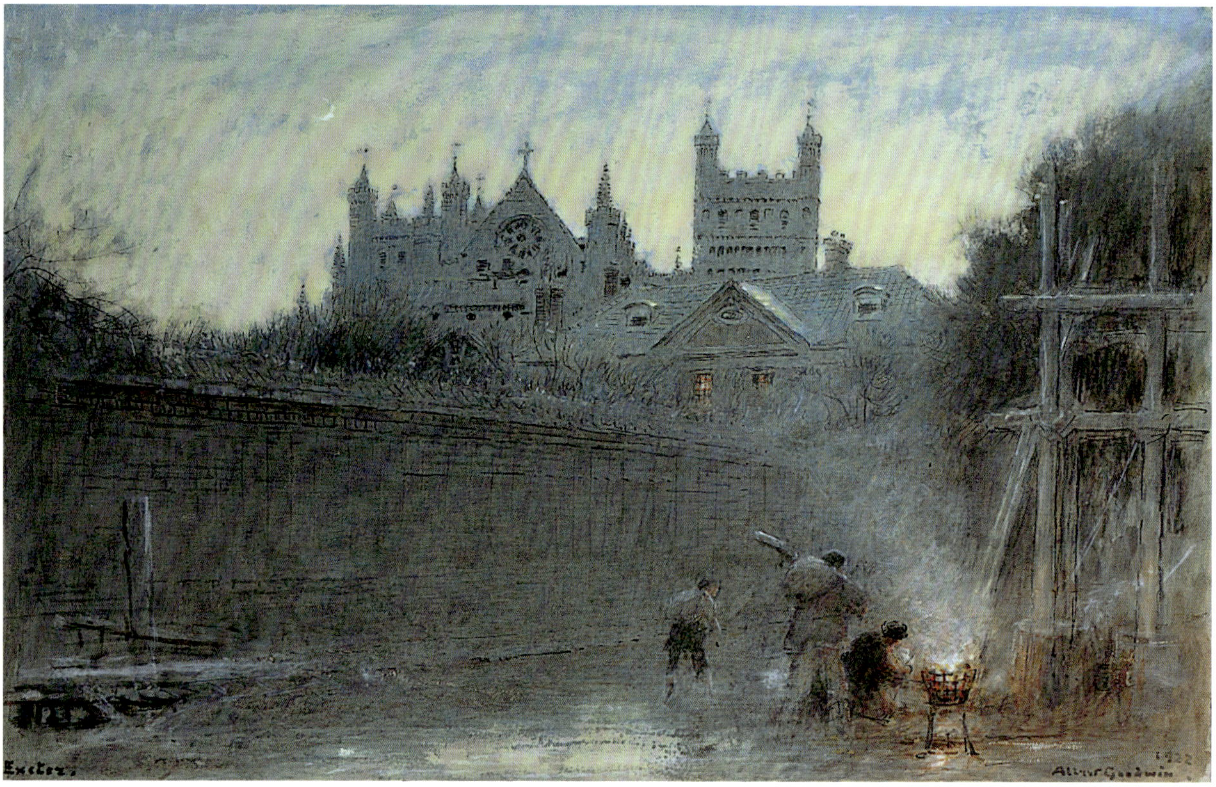

'I have been fortunate enough to survive until now, and have thought it wise with the knowledge gained by maturity deliberately to do things I have done before, avoiding the pitfalls and places of stumbling which I generally fell into. I may be mistaken in thinking I have had a little success in this, but the "show" must be my judge for better or for worse.

I have had continual pleasure in doing them. The ever-changing aspect of the world, openings of fresh astonishments, and wonders to the landscape painter, the longer he lives making his art to be ever renewing its youth, and discovering to him that even in Bolshevism there may be something of truth, if it only teaches him what to avoid.'

Albert Goodwin, *Diary, 1922*

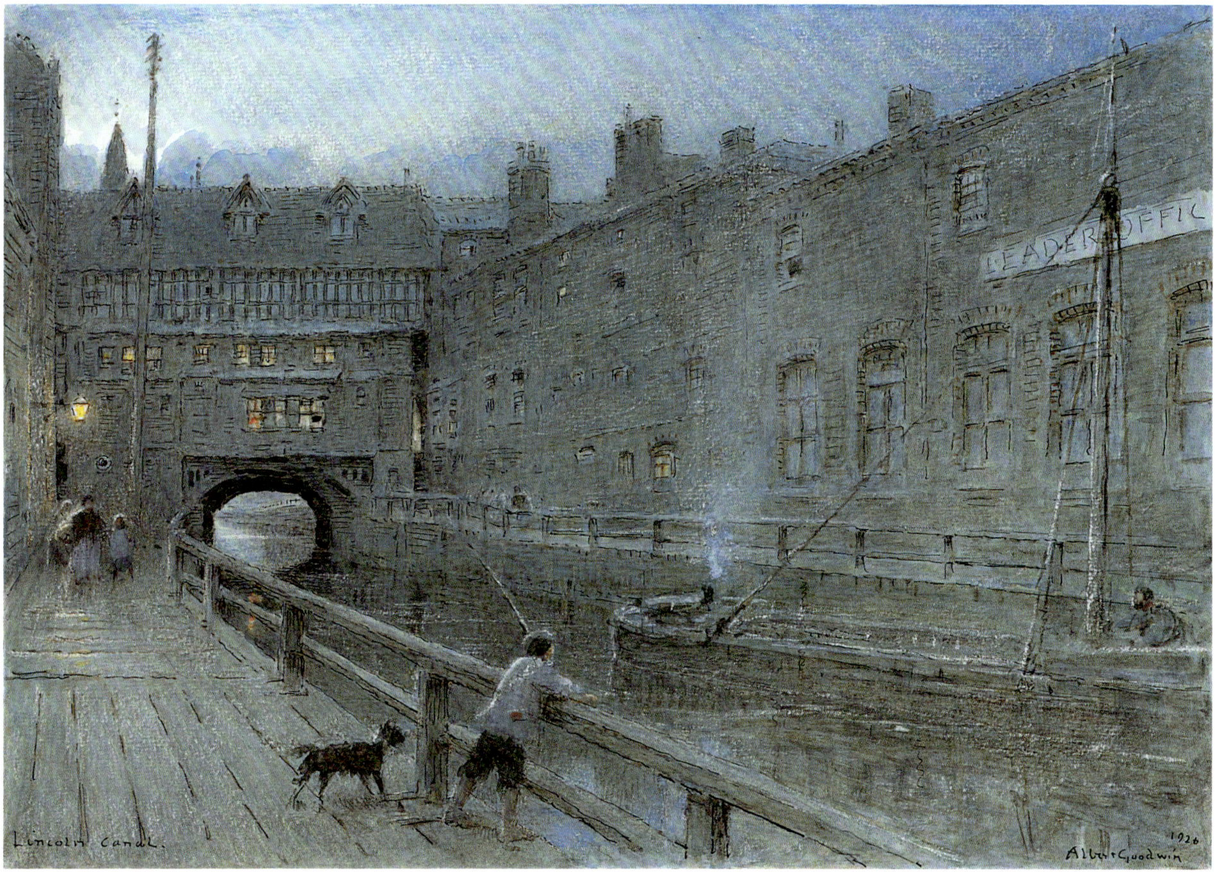

124 LINCOLN CANAL
signed, inscribed with title and dated 1926
watercolour with bodycolour
and pen and ink
10 x 14 ¼ INCHES

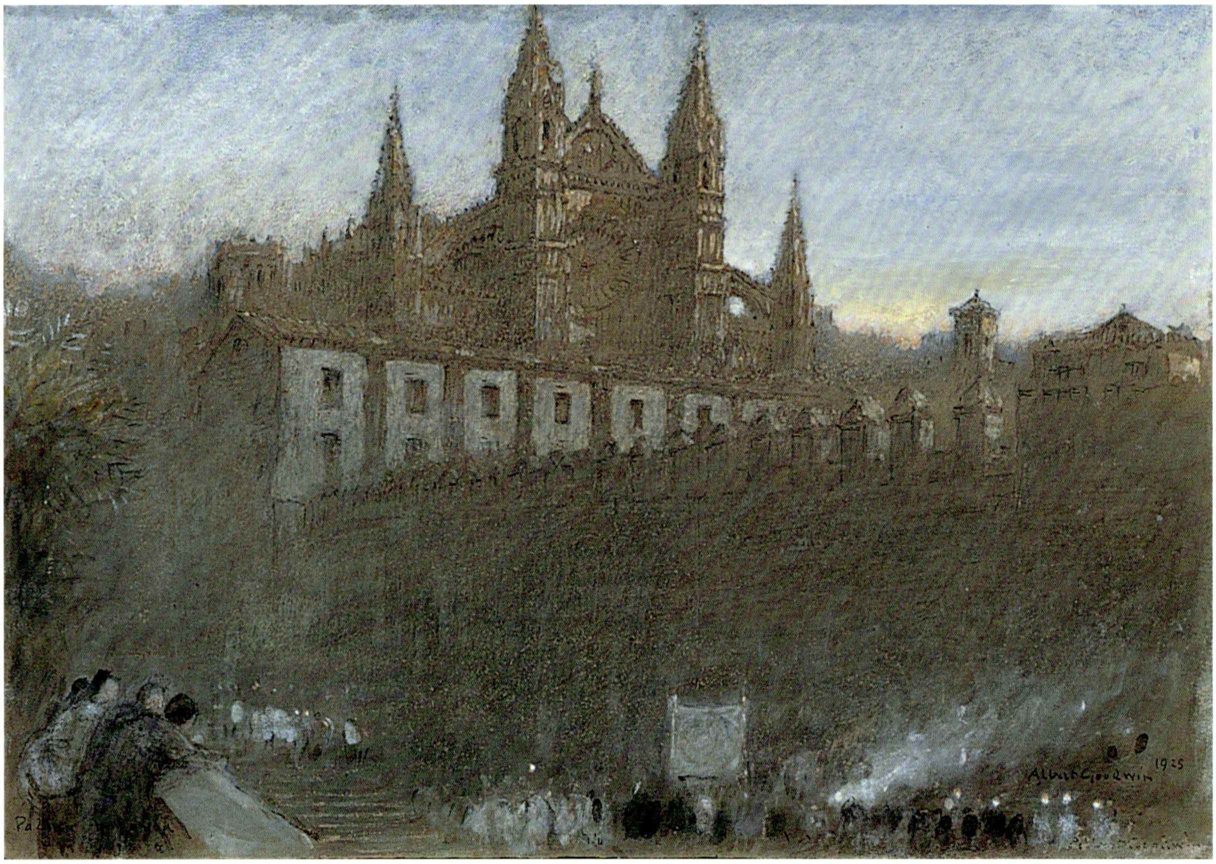

125 PALMA MAJORCA

signed, inscribed with title twice and dated 1925

watercolour with pen and ink

9 ½ x 14 INCHES

126 SYRACUSE

signed, inscribed with title and dated 1926

pen and ink

7 x 10 INCHES

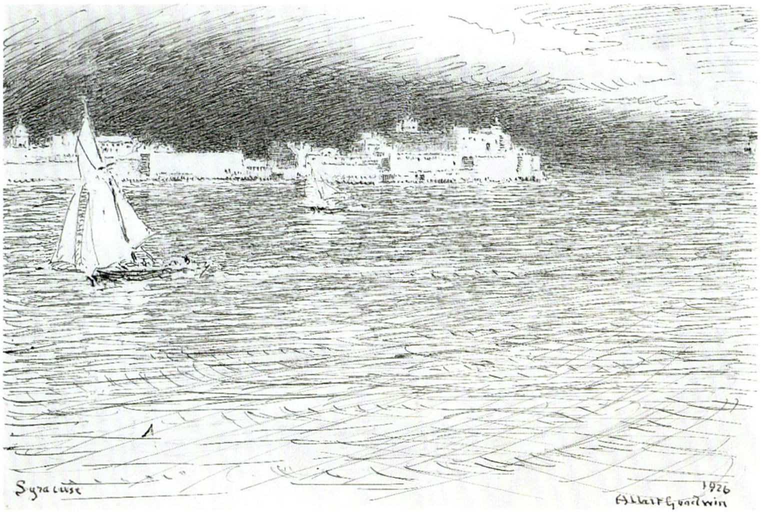

127 PALMA MAJORCA (back endpapers)

signed, inscribed with title and dated 1925

watercolour with pen and ink

10 ½ x 14 ½ INCHES

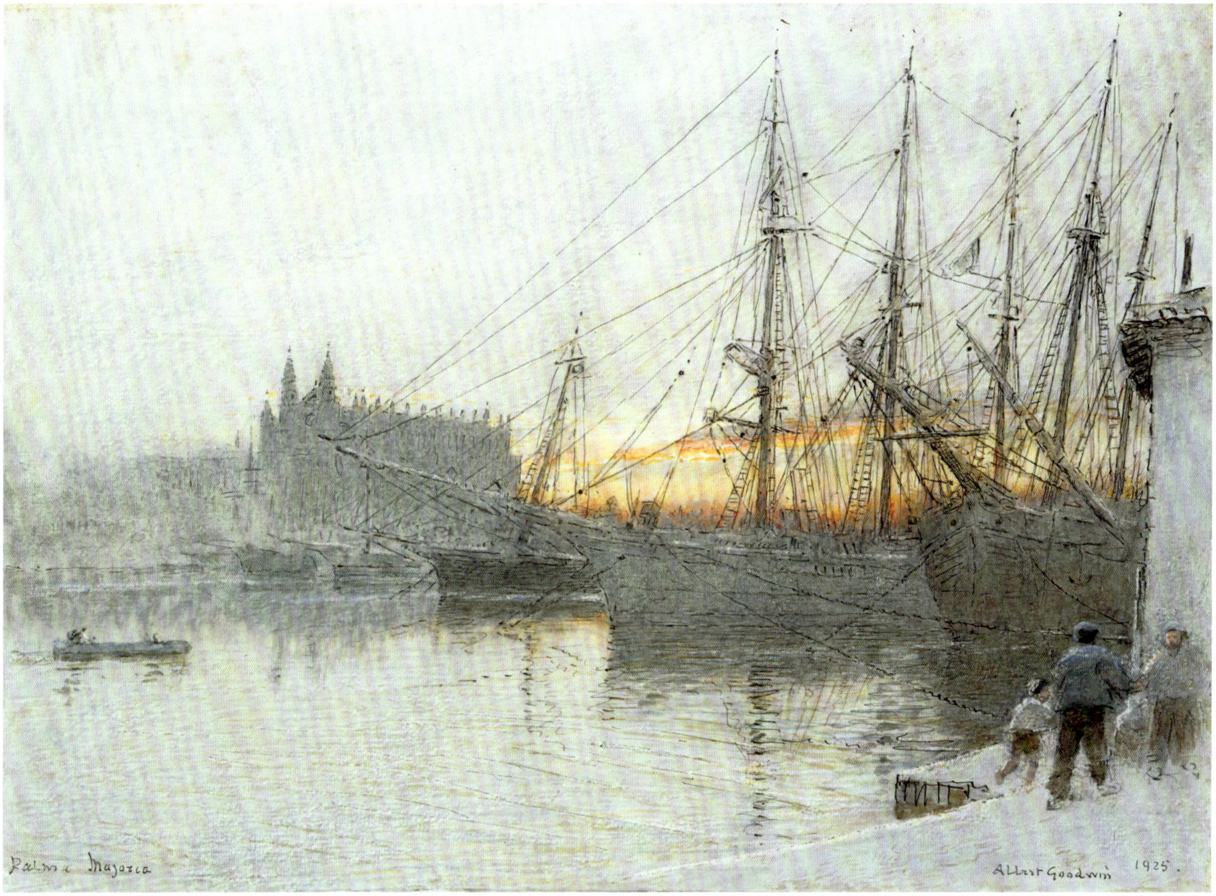

HARRY GOODWIN (1842-1926)

An elder brother of Albert Goodwin, Harry Goodwin was born in Maidstone, Kent. He married Kate Malleson, and together they lived in various places in southern England, including Brighton, Croydon, Hastings and Torquay. As a painter of landscapes, genre and still life in oil and watercolour, he exhibited from 1867 at such leading institutions as the Royal Academy, the Royal Institute of Painters in Oils and the Royal Institute of Painters in Water-Colours. He also had solo shows at Walker's Galleries in 1921 and 1924, and at least one at Dickinson's Galleries. In the year that he illustrated W A Knight's *Through the Wordsworth Country* (1887) he accompanied Albert on a trip to Lucerne and the Italian Lakes. He would return to Italy in 1892 and 1920.

128 A SUNDRENCHED VALLEY (opposite)
signed with monogram and dated 1918
watercolour with bodycolour
13 x 20 INCHES

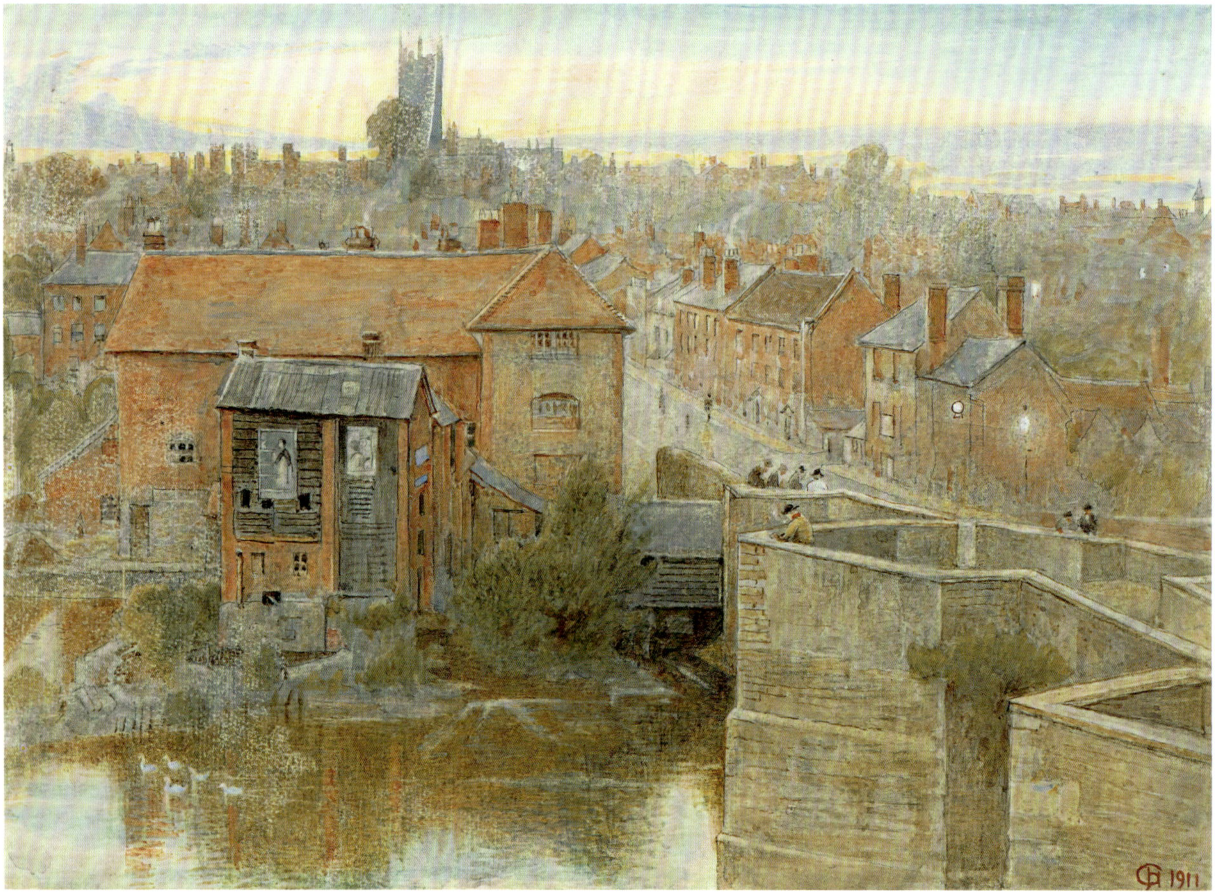

129 LUDLOW
signed with monogram and dated 1911
watercolour with bodycolour
10 x 14 INCHES

A picture with this title was exhibited at Dickinson's Galleries, as no 10 (priced at £21), though the date of the show is unknown; it appeared with the tag 'Milton's "Comus" was first performed here in the year 1634'.

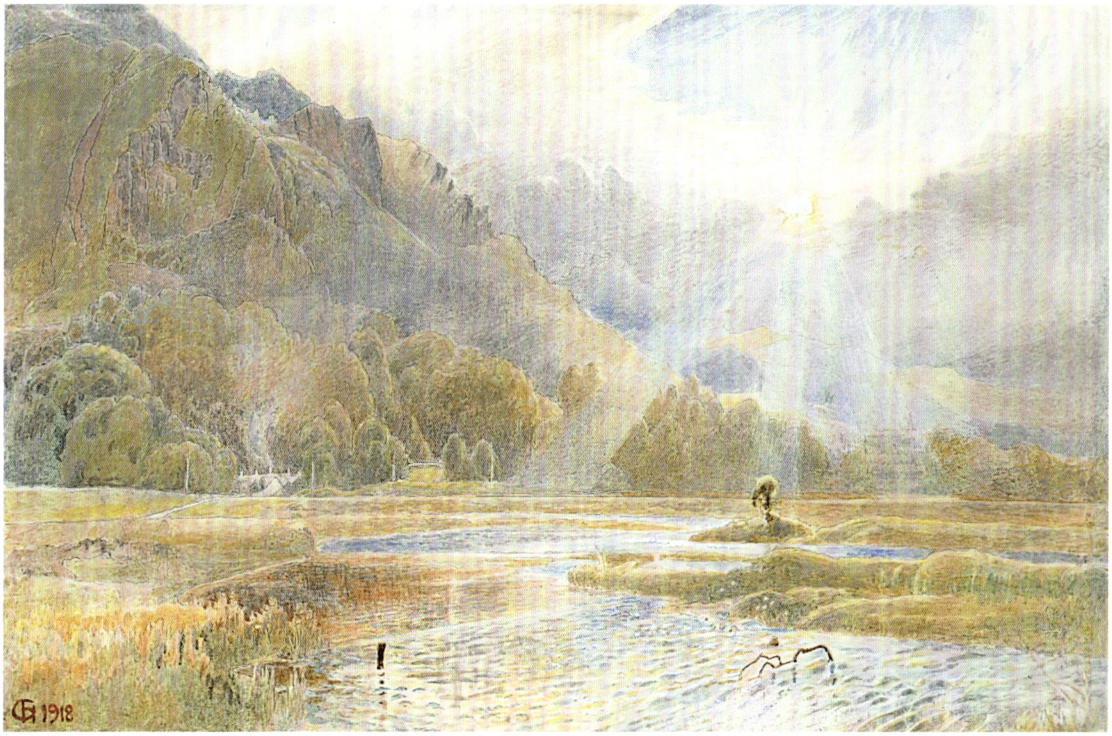

KATE MALLESON GOODWIN (ACTIVE 1862-1900)

Kate Malleson of Croydon married Harry Goodwin. A painter of landscapes, flower pieces and portraits, she exhibited at the Royal Academy between 1873 and 1893, while one painting, *The Old Rookery, Winchelsea*, was included in an exhibition of Goodwin family members held at Maidstone Museum and Art Gallery in 1879. In about 1887 it seems that Ruskin commissioned her to produce a series of copies of Carpaccio's cycle of St Ursula paintings that hang in the Accademia in Venice.

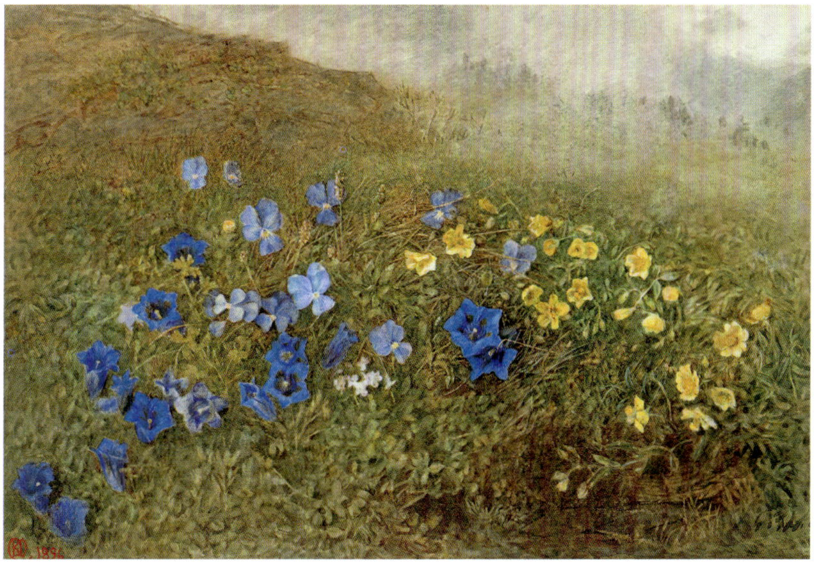

130 SPRING MOUNTAIN FLOWERS

signed with monogram and dated 1896

watercolour

11 ½ x 17 ½ INCHES

not illustrated

131 FIELDS UNDER PILATUS IN SPRING TIME

signed with monogram and dated 1893

watercolour

12 ¼ x 18 inches

ALBERT GOODWIN – CHRONOLOGY

1845	17 JANUARY: born at 62 Boxley Road, Maidstone, seventh child of Samuel Goodwin, builder, and Rosetta. Educated at Mr Weekstead's school in Bedford Place. Apprenticed to a Maidstone draper. Met William Holman Hunt and Arthur Hughes and in early 1860s became pupil of Ford Madox Brown. Exhibited first painting at the Royal Academy: *Under the Hedge*, no 156. Visited Jersey and Holland.
BY 1867	Living in Arundel, at The Parade. Married his first wife, Mary Ann Lucas, aged 24, of Arundel on 16 February 1867. She died on the 13 December 1869. The death certificate records her age then as 30 and the cause of death tubercular peritonitis.
1870–77	Living in London at 2 Finborough Road, Fulham. Sketching holiday with Ruskin in Abingdon and later in Matlock where they were joined by Arthur Severn. Elected Associate of the Royal Society of Painters in Water-Colours (ARWS). Travelled to Italy with Ruskin and Severn.
1873	To Switzerland, staying three months at the village of Simplon. Visited Egypt with his second wife, Alice Desborough. EASTER: visited Holland and Belgium including Dordrecht, Bruges and Ypres. Elected full member of the Royal Society of Painters in Water-Colours (RWS).
1888	To Locarno, Switzerland.
1889	To Locarno, Switzerland.
1892	To Norway.
1893	To India.
1900	MARCH: to southern Italy, including Torre del Greco.
1902	JANUARY: sailed to the West Indies, returning via Niagara and North America, as the guest of Arthur McConnell.
1906	Moved to 'Ellerslie', Bexhill-on-Sea.
1907	To Lucerne, Switzerland.
1909	JANUARY: to Egypt staying in Cairo and Suez. APRIL: to Switzerland, visiting Baveno, Lago Maggiore, Fribourg, Berne, Lucerne and Engelberg.

1910 AUGUST: to Switzerland, visiting Launterbrunnen and Spiez, Lake Thun.

1911 MAY: to Switzerland, visiting Weggis, Lake Lucerne and Engelberg.

1912 JANUARY: to the West Indies, again as a guest of Arthur McConnell. Returned via North America.

1913 JUNE: to Switzerland, visiting Pontresina and Schaffhausen.

1914 MAY: to Italy, visiting Naples, Palermo and Taormina.

JULY: to Switzerland, visiting Geneva and Chamonix.

1916 11 JANUARY: death of his wife Alice.

NOVEMBER: sailed to New Zealand and Australia.

1917 Visited Sicily as a guest of Sir Thomas Devitt.

1918 17 APRIL: 'To my astonishment had an intimation from the secretary RWS that two of my drawings sold on the PV day. This was most surprising as I risked putting full pre-War prices on them. This makes three gone out of my six, for *Benares* was sold (and paid for) before it went in. It seems as though I cannot be ruined and bankrupt - not even by the war. Someone tells me that he overheard at the same PV two men talking over *Benares* and one said, "Goodwin is a lucky man, he has many friends who invited him to go abroad and that accounts for the great variety of his subjects." I shall be known perhaps by and by as "The variety Artist," but there is a measure of truth in this overheard remark. I certainly have been lucky, and it is true that luck has helped me considerably about the world, and in a most pleasant, not to say friendly, way. Last by no means least was my visit (as guest of Sir Thomas Devlin) to Sicily, who indeed was the one who heard the gossip, and have had a chuckle about it.'

1932 10 APRIL: died, aged 87.

Chris Beetles has mounted a number of important and successful exhibitions on Albert Goodwin. These include:

Albert Goodwin RWS 1845-1932: 129 of his best works borrowed from private collections, 1986, which toured to the Bankside Gallery, London; the Mappin Art Gallery, Sheffield; and Stoke-on-Trent City Museum and Art Gallery. This was accompanied by two publications: an illustrated catalogue, and a sumptuous limited edition volume of 1,000, with 450 pages and over 200 colour plates, measuring 12 x 16 inches and quarter bound in leather by Zaehndorfs with top edge gilt, blocking and slip cased.

Albert Goodwin RWS 1845-1932, 1996. This exhibition was also accompanied by a large full-colour illustrated catalogue with 128 pages and extracts from Goodwin's diaries.

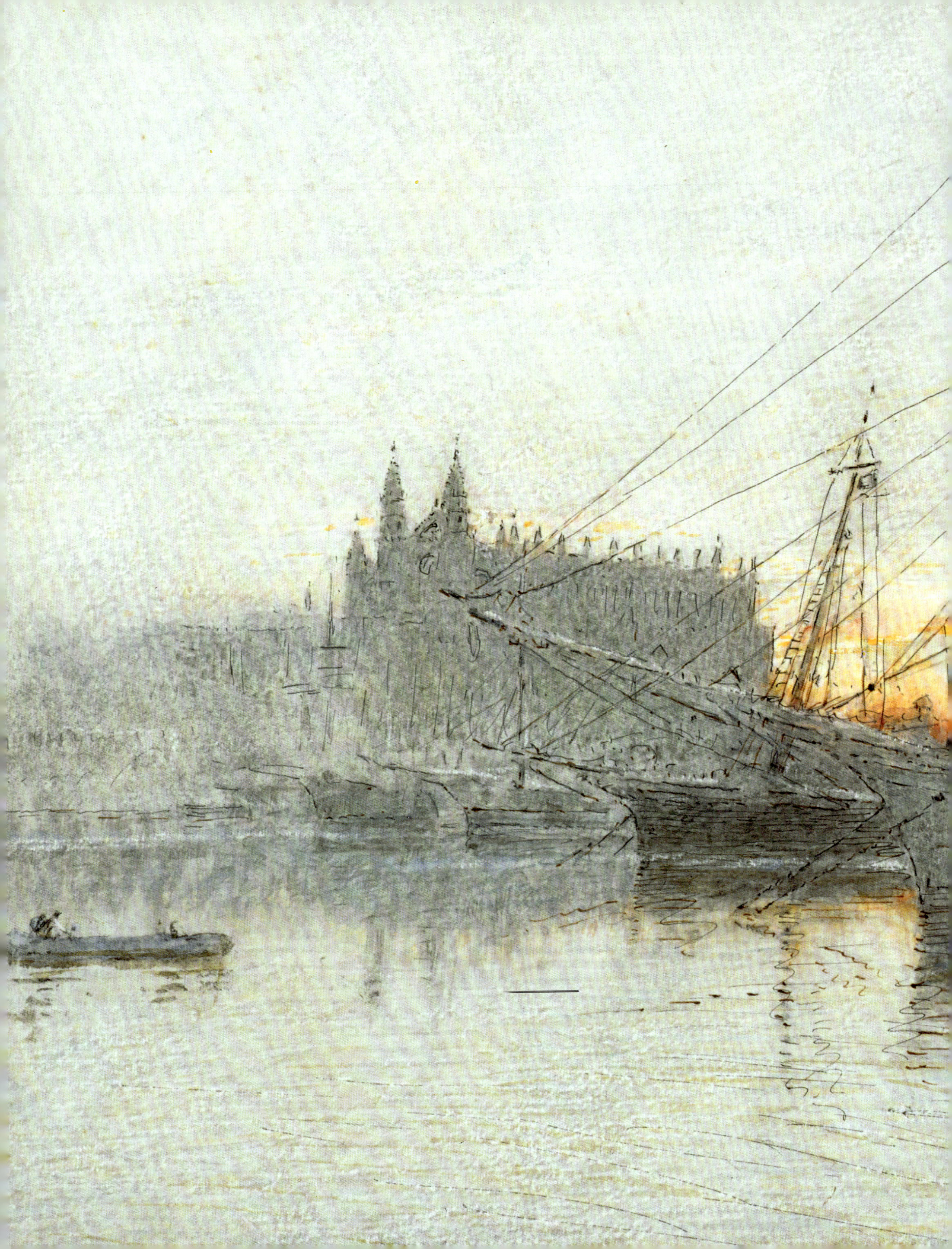